The Story of Sitka

The Historic Outpost of the Northwest Coast

The Chief Factory of the Russian American Company

by

C. L. Andrews

Contents

SITKA
Foreword

The panorama of sea, island, and mountain, which holds Sitka, Alaska, as a jewel in its setting, is one of the most beautiful of those which surround the cities of the world. Toward the sea from the peninsula on which Sitka is situated stretches an expanse of waters, studded with forest-clad islands which break the swell of the Pacific that foams and tumbles on the outer barriers. To the westward Mount Edgecumbe lifts its perfect cone, its summit truncated by the old crater whose fires have been dead for centuries; to the northward Harbor peak lifts its signal to mariners; the Sisters, with a gleam of snow and ice among their pinnacles, lie in the distance of Indian River; to the east is the arrowhead of Mount Verstovia; the glaciers glisten beyond; and the sweep of mist-clad mountains, in their softness, beyond the bay to the southeast completes the circle.

Radiating like the spokes of a wheel, waterways with historic memories reach out from the town. Krestof Bay, where the early navigators cast anchor; Neva Strait, commemorating the first Russian ship that visited Sitka from around the world; Katleanski Bay, on which was situated Old Sitka; Silver Bay, a Norwegian fjord transplanted to Alaska; Lisianski Bay, named for the Russian navigator of a century ago; the inlet at Ozerskoe Redoubt and Globokoe (Deep) Lake; the island-studded way to the Hot Springs; each with its individual charm; the ocean, with the deep, rich, marine tints of northern waters; the forest of blue, that folds like a robe over the mountains; the mountain summits beside the glaciers, clad in the exquisitely wonderful green of the Northland, all are delightful. But when the sun sinks low in the west, with the long, lingering twilight of the North, and the soft, delicate rays touch and blend with the water and islands, the mountains and sky–then, in the mystery of the evening, is the supreme beauty of the land. To those who have really known and loved Sitka, there is no place on earth to compare.

There are pleasant recollections of those who have lived there. Jovial Edward Degroff and his stories at the Roastology Club; the Mills, whose hospitable home is known to every resident of the town; Wm. Gouverneur Morris, whose name recalls a leader of Revolutionary days; genial George Barron, who upheld every good tradition of the Navy; the gallant old soldier, Matthew P. Berry; dignified Judge Delaney, Alaska's staunchest advocate through all vicissitudes; Governor Brady, with his neverfailing faith in Alaska's greatness; Captain Francis, without whom the early naval commanders thought the warships could not thread the intricate passages; Nicholas Haley, with his optimistic dreams of El Doradoes; Pauline Archangelsky, for whom the "Old Timers" have pleasant recollections; Alonzo Austin and his mission; Captain Kilgore of the "Rush"; Merrill, who caught on the photograph plate the elusive spirit of the varying surroundings as only a true artist could; Katherine Delaney Abrams, whose touch in watercolor delineated the glory of the sunsets as none else could; Professor Richardson, who for a quarter of a century returned year after year thousands of miles to perpetuate in paintings the exquisite tintings of glaciers and mountain; George Kostromitinoff (Father Sergius); Father Metropolski, and many others who have made a part of the quaint old town.

There is a saying that whosoever comes to love the waters of the Indian River will ever after yearn for them, and it seems true, for always is that harking back to its banks with an unsatisfied longing.

From prehistoric time this has been the home of the Sitka Kwan of the Thlingit people. For sixty-three years it was the scene of the chief activities of the Russian American Company, who represented the rule of the Muscovites, who, when Chicago was but a blockhouse in a sedgy swamp on the banks of a sluggish, reedy river, and when San Francisco was but a mission and a Presidio of sunburned bricks, maintained in Sitka a community of busy people who were casting cannon and bells, and who were building ships for commerce.

In the establishment of this outpost the foundation was laid for the title of the United States to the southeastern part of Alaska, a land rich in fur and forest, in gold and copper, in marble and fish, the potential possibilities of which are not even approximately forecasted today. Enough to say of it, that in its limits are two mines, one of which has yielded over sixty-five millions of dollars in gold, and the other ranks among the richest of the mineral producing veins of the world.

Some may have an interest in the story of the quaint, quiet, beautiful village on the shore of Baranof Island. I hope this may add something to history, keeping the events of the past bright in the memory of those who love the Northland and its story, and add a little of interest and information of the present to those who come as transient visitors to while away a few days among the myriad islands of the Sitkan Archipelago. It is a link to connect the Sitka of the past, the *Novo Arkangelsk* of the great Russian American Company in the romantic days of the fur trade when it was the center of the vast domain of Russian America and gathered to its magazines the pelts of sea-otter and fox, with the Sitka of today with its fisheries and mines. The old landmarks are fast disappearing, scarce a year passes without some monument passing away, and even their location will soon be forgotten unless some record is made for those who do not know where they stood.

CHAPTER I
DISCOVERY

Sitka of the Russians, a century ago, was the center of trade and civilization on the Northwest Coast of America, the chief factory of the Russian American Company in the vast and little known land of the Russian Possessions in America. The sails of ships from far off Kronstadt on the Baltic brought Russian cargoes. The famous clipper ships of New England made it a stopping place on their way to the China seas. English traders and explorers visited it on their voyages, and in it was centered the trade of a wide region. It was the chief factory of the greatest rival in the fur trade of the world, with which the Honourable, the Hudson's Bay Company, which then was the controlling power in the English fur market, had to contend.

The story of Sitka goes back past the middle of the Eighteenth Century. There are Russians, Spanish, English, French and Americans who have woven each their own part of the web of the tale, and the scenes have been as varied and strange as the people.

July 16, 1741, a Russian ship stood into a broad harbor on the Northwest Coast of America. The commander, Captain Alexei Chirikof, had sailed three thousand miles across the unknown Pacific from the shores of the Okhotsk Sea. Civilized eyes had never before rested on these shores and he was keen with the excitement of adventure and discovery as he dropped anchor. He sent a party ashore in the ship's longboat to explore, and awaited the result. Days passed and no word or signal came, so the remaining boat was sent to recall the party and it was swallowed up in the labyrinth among the green islands. Signals indicated that it safely landed but none returned to the ship although the orders were imperative that both boats return at once. The last boat was gone. Three weeks passed. Captain Chirikof could not reach the shore and could no longer lie at anchor, so reluctantly and sadly he set his course for the far off Kamchatkan shores and sailed away from the port of missing men.

Lovers' Lane, Sitka.

Nearly two centuries have passed since the Russian seamen landed and no word has come from them. For more than seventy years the Russian Government sought for some sign of their fate.[1] Tales were told of a colony of Russians existing on the coast but each upon investigation proved but a rumor.

There is a dim tradition among the Sitkas of men being lured ashore in the long ago. They say that Chief Annahootz, the predeces-

---

[1] January 20th, 1820, a letter written by the Directory at St. Petersburg to Chief Manager Muravief at Sitka enclosing instructions previously given to Hagemeister, instructing him to find the descendants of Chirikof's lost men, urging that it must be done, and expressing surprise that it had been neglected thus long. (Russian American Archives, Correspondence, Vol. II, No. 108.)

sor of the chief of that name who was the firm friend of the whites at Sitka in 1878, was the leading actor in the tragedy. Annahootz dressed himself in the skin of a bear and played along the beach. So skillfully did he simulate the sinuous motions of the animal that the Russians in the excitement of the chase plunged into the woods in pursuit and there the savage warriors killed them to a man, leaving none to tell the story. The disappearance of Chirikof's men has remained one of the many unsolved mysteries of the Northland, and their fate will never be known to a certainty.

The faulty record of the navigation of a time that counted by dead reckoning, and without a knowledge of the currents of those seas, does not tell us the exact location of the anchorage, but beyond a reasonable doubt it was in Sitka Sound, and the Russian seamen died at the hands of the Sitka Kwan of the Thlingits. In this manner Sitka first became known to the White Man's World.

On the 16th day of August, 1775, came the Royal Standard of Spain, flung to the breeze from the little schooner "Sonora," only 36 feet in length, under command of Don Francisco de la Bodega y Quadra. Quadra was one of the greatest and best of the Spanish navigators in the North. His voyages are among the most successful of those of the mariners of his nation in the waters of the north Pacific ocean, and his name was once linked with that of the English Commander on the island now bearing the name of Vancouver. Quadra came from the Mexican port of San Blas, and after many thrilling adventures and grievous hardships he sailed into a broad bay and dropped anchor. There was a mountain, of which he says: "Of the most regular and beautiful form I had ever seen. It was also quite detached from the great ridge of mountains. Its top was covered with snow, under which appeared some gullies, which continue till about the middle of the mountain, and from thence to the bottom are trees of the same kind as those at Trinity."

He named the mountain *San Jacinthus*, and the point of the island that extends out toward the sea, Cape *del Engano*. No one who has looked upon the slopes of the mountain which stands to the seaward from Sitka can mistake the description. He anchored in what is now known as Krestof Bay, about six miles northwest from Sitka, and he called it Port *Guadalupe*.

Mount Edgecumbe.

Captain Cook, on his Third Voyage of Exploration, in 1778, with the ships "Resolution" and "Discovery," passed along the coast and noted the bay, of which he says: "An arm of this bay, in the northern part of it, seemed to extend in toward the north, behind a round elevated mountain I called Mount Edgecumbe, and the point of land that shoots out from it Cape Edgecumbe." This name supplanted the one given by the Spaniard and the beautiful cone is yet known by the title he bestowed.

The early Russians called the mountain St. Lazaria, assuming that it was the peak seen by Chirikof on his ill fated voyage of discovery and so named by him. The small island at the south is still known as San Lazaria Island.

Captain Dixon, of H. M. S. "Queen Charlotte," came during the summer of 1787, on a fur trading voyage. Dixon had just departed from the harbor when Captain Portlock, of the English ship "King George," which was lying in Portlock Harbor, to the northward in Chichagoff Island, sent his ship's boat through the passage behind Kruzof Island to about the present site of Sitka, and made the discovery for the civilized world that Mount Edgecumbe is on an island.

7

CHAPTER II
SETTLEMENT

The sea-otter, a marine animal about four feet in length when fully grown, with soft, long black pelage of silky texture, is one of the most valued of the fur-bearers. It was found abundantly all the way along the Northwest Coast, and especially in the passages about Sitka. It is now nearly extinct.

The Russians had been gathering the skins of the sea-otter in the northern waters for years, ever since Chirikof made his voyage to Sitka, and they were truly an El Dorado, in fur, to the traders who plied their trade along the coasts. Captain Cook and his sailors, when on their voyage in these waters, bought skins for mere trifles, some for a handful of iron nails. These same skins sold for as much as sixty dollars each in China where they visited on their way home. The story of the furs went over the world and English, French and American traders thronged to these waters to sail their ships into the straits and barter for the rich pelts. To secure a profit of $50,000 on a voyage was not unusual. Ingraham, the lieutenant of Captain Gray whom we all know so well for his discovery of the great River of the West, sailed to near Sitka before his principal entered the river which he named for his ship, the Columbia. The French ship "Solide," in 1791, sailed from France to gather a portion of the harvest. Her captain, Étienne Marchand, anchored in Sitka Bay, and called it *Tchinkitinay*, as he declares it was known to the natives. To his ship flocked the painted and skin-clad natives with their peltries for barter. On their persons he saw articles of European manufacture, showing that other ships had visited there, and in the ears of one young savage were hanging pendant two copper coins of the colony of Massachusetts. His success in trade was not such as he might have wished, so he sailed way, remarking that, "The modern Hebrews would, perhaps, have little to teach to these people in the art of trade."

March 31st, 1799, the Yankee skipper, Cleveland, of the merchant ship "Caroline," sailed into the bay, dropped anchor and fired a cannon shot as a signal. He was one of those shrewd, lean traders, skilled in navigation, who sailed from Boston round the Horn, with their bucko mates, who could drive a tack with the prow of a ship, so to speak, and in those days there were no corners of the earth where they might not be found seeking for profit. He was wise to the ways of the sharp trading canoemen of these waters, and their aggressive proclivities, so he prepared his ship with regard for all the possibilities of the business. Around it as a bulwark he stretched a barrier of dry bull hides brought from the California coast. At the stern was a place prepared for the trading. Forward on the deck were planted cannon, shotted with shrapnel, trained so as to rake the afterdeck, and beside each was a gunner's match.

On the first day, for two hundred yards of broadcloth, he purchased a hundred prime sea-otter skins, worth $50 each in Canton. Barter was going merrily on, when a scream from amidships startled the crew. The Thlingits sprang to their boats. The squaws backed the canoes away from the ship's sides. Arrows were fitted to bowstrings, spears were poised and muskets primed. On the ships the sailors lighted the cannon matches and stood by ready to fire. A fight was hovering in the air when the cause of the disturbance was discovered. An inquisitive Thlingit pried between the bull hides opposite the cook's galley, and the cook had saluted him with a ladle of hot water. In his surprise he upset his canoe and his family were struggling in the sea. His baby was rescued by a seaman, amends were made to his injured feelings, and the barter proceeded as before.

The waters were filled with ships. In a stay of a month the "Caroline" spoke the ship "Hancock," the ship "Despatch," the ship "Ulysses," and the ship "Eliza," all of Boston; and the English ship "Cheerful," all trading for furs among the Sitkan Islands.

The Russians, in their colony on Kodiak Island, were jealous of the intruders on what they considered as their domain. Gregory Shelikof, a Siberian merchant, one of the wealthiest and most far seeing of the leaders among the Aleutian Islands, conceived the plan of combining the whole of the fur trade in one great monopoly. In pursuance of this policy he secured a charter from Emperor Paul in 1799, under the name of the Russian American Company, which gave the exclusive right to all profits to be derived from every form of resource in the Russian possessions in America for a period of twenty years. To the management of his business in the Colony he established on Kodiak Island he appointed Alexander Andreevich Baranof, a Siberian trader of great ability and experience. Baranof, the wise and far-seeing Russian ruler of the Russian American Company, at his factory in St. Paul's Harbor on Kodiak Island, had long planned the extension of his settlements to the southeast. The sea-otter catch of the Russians was made by brigades of Aleuts from the western islands, who went along the shores and to sea as far as 20 miles, in their wonderful skin boats called bidarkas, to hunt. When a sea-otter lifted its head from the water to breathe, within sight of a detachment of Aleut hunters, its fate was sealed, for it seldom escaped.

The passages between the islands about Sitka were called the "Straits" by the Russians, and in them the sea-otter skins were taken by the thousands. It was not unusual for a Russian hunting party consisting of a hundred bidarkas to take on one expedition 2,000 skins of the *Morski bobrov*, as they called the sea-otter.

The animals were becoming scarce in the seas about the western islands and Baranof was compelled to replenish his trade by the catch of the southeastern waters. In 1795 he sent one of his ships as far south as the Queen Charlotte Islands and it visited Sitka on the way. Two thousand skins were secured by the hunters while on this voyage. In the same year Baranof himself paid Sitka a visit, coming through the strait from the north in his little schooner "Olga," a 40-foot boat, and he named the passage for his craft as Olga Strait. On the shore near his anchorage he erected a cross; the bay he named Krestof Bay, and he then selected the locality of his future settlement.

In the spring of 1799, Baranof sent orders to the toyons, or chiefs, of the tribes on the islands around Kodiak to assemble the hunters. Five hundred and fifty bidarkas, each manned by from two to three Aleut paddlers, came in answer to his call, and with two convoying ships he set sail for Sitka Sound. On July 7th he landed at a bay six miles north of the present town of Sitka, purchased a tract of land from Skayeutlelt, a local chief, and began the construction of a post which he named redoubt St. Michael. The building was done under great difficulties. Rain fell incessantly. There were but thirty Russian workmen as most of the Aleuts returned to Kodiak, hunting as they went. Of the men who remained ten had to stand guard constantly, for the Thlingits were not to be trusted. Barracks, storehouses, quarters for the commanding officer, were constructed; a bath house also, for the Russian must have his bath, and the whole was surrounded by a stockade and strengthened by blockhouses. Their troubles were not all with the elements, for during the winter the scarcity of provision and other causes brought scurvy to add to their discomfort. Their food was mostly yu-hali (dried salmon), but during the winter the hunters took 40 sea-lions, and in the spring many seals were killed in the bay by the Aleuts.

The natives, called Thlingits at the present, were known as the Kolosh by the Russians. They were divided among themselves in their feelings toward the new settlers in their midst. Some looked with extreme disfavor upon the establishment, while others were friendly. The young and turbulent warriors were hostile. A messenger was sent to invite them to a prasdnik (holiday) at the fort. He was taken prisoner by them and detained until Baranof landed in their midst with an armed force and demanded his release, when they set him free and ridiculed the incident. At a dance at the fort many of the Kolosh came with long knives concealed under their cloaks. Their treachery was detected and their design frustrated. The courage and caution of Baranof held them in check until spring when he departed for Kodiak, leaving strict instructions as to the precautions to be observed during his absence. After his departure the discipline grew more lax and the Kolosh became more bold. The watchful savages at last saw an opportunity to rid themselves of their new neighbors.

On a June day of 1802, the exact date is not recorded, a horde of painted savages burst from the forest, clad in all the paraphernalia of war masks and barbaric armour. A fleet of war canoes landed warriors on the beach in front of the redoubt. In the attack that followed the stockade and buildings were reduced to smoking ruins, the magazines were robbed of rich stores of furs, most of the defenders died on the spears of the Kolosh or were tortured till death relieved their sufferings, and the women and children were made slaves. Skayeutlelt, the false friend of Baranof, directed the battle from a nearby knoll and his nephew, Katlean, was one of the principal actors in the bloody tragedy. A few survivors who were hunting in their bidarkas or were in the forest, escaped to the ships of the English and American traders which were in the bay.

Captain Ebbetts on an American ship and Captain Barber of the British ship "Myrtle" were in the harbor. Some of the survivors on reaching these ships asked them to rescue their countrymen. Captain Ebbetts ransomed several prisoners, but Captain Barber adopted a more effective course. Chief Katlean and Chief Skayeutlelt came on board his ship to trade. He at once put them in irons and threatened to hang them to the yardarm of the ship if the captives remaining in the hands of the natives, and also the plundered sea-otter skins, were not immediately surrendered to him. The threat was effective, the greater part of the sea-otter furs and several captives were brought on the ship and delivered to him. He then took the ransomed captives from the other ship and sailed for Kodiak, where he demanded a ransom of 50,000 rubles from Baranof for the captives. The ransom was later reduced to 10,000 rubles which was paid by Mr. Baranof.

Two years passed before much is again known of Sitka. English and American captains sailed their ships into the harbor and gathered the furs which Baranof had endeavored to garner in the storehouses of the Russian American Company. In the summer of 1804 Baranof gathered a force at Kodiak with which to cross the Gulf of Alaska to re-establish his post. There were one hundred and fifty bearded *promyshileniks*, or fur hunters, and over 500 Aleuts in their skin bidarkas. With him were the ships "Alexander," "Ekaterina," "Yermak," and "Rostislaf." When they reached Sitka they found there Captain Lisianski of the Imperial Russian Navy, with the ship "Neva," one of the first Russians to circle the globe, and who came to help to recapture the post.

The Indian village of Sitka was almost in the same place as the present town, grouped around the Baranof hill which was called by the Russians a *kekoor*. On the top of the kekoor was a redoubt, and a stronger fort was near the mouth of the Indian River, or *Kolosh Ryeku*.

On the morning of September 28th the Russian ships moved to a point opposite the village, the "Neva" being towed by a hundred bidarkas. The Sitkans abandoned their village and the fort on the hill and withdrew to the stronger fortification near the river. Baranof landed a force and occupied the kekoor, planted cannon on the top, then opened negotiations for the surrender of the other fort, but his overtures were rejected by the Indians.

The ships were brought near the river fort and the cannon were trained on it. The fort was built of thick logs in the shape of an irregular square, with portholes on the side next the sea, and inside the breast works were 14 barabaras, or native houses.

The walls were of such thickness that the cannon shot from the "Neva" made but little impression on the structure. Baranof was impatient and urged an attack. Reinforcements were landed from the ships under command of Lieutenants Arbusof and Polavishin. The hunters, sailors, and Aleuts flung themselves against the fortifications, but meeting a murderous fire were driven back in disorder and only saved from disaster by the protection of the fire of the ships. Ten men were killed and 26 wounded, and among the wounded was Baranof.

Captain Lisianski then took command and moved his ships nearer the shore. A canoe with reinforcements and a supply of powder for the Indians approached among the islands but a shot from the "Neva" struck it, the powder exploded, and the Indians who were saved from the wreck were taken on board the Russian ship. The bombardment was steadily continued until the 6th of October, when the Kolosh proposed to surrender, and a parley was held, but during the night they evacuated the fort and went over the mountains to the north. In the fort were left the bodies of 30 warriors and also the bodies of five children who had been killed to prevent their cries making the retreat known to the Russians. The only remaining survivors were two old women and a little boy. A few straggling warriors remained lurking about, seeking revenge, and a few days later they killed eight Aleuts who were fishing on Jamestown Bay.

How the Kolosh went over the mountains was long a mystery to the Russians. They reached the shore of Peril Strait and crossing to the north shore placed a fort near the entrance to Sitkoh Bay which was stronger than their old fort at Indian River and where over 1,000 people gathered. A tradition among the old Indians says that the fugitives first went to Old Sitka, then over the mountains to the northeastern side of the island. On the way they suffered extremely from fatigue and hunger, and one Sitka Indian who lives on Peril Strait relates that his father was a child at the time of the exodus. His father carried him till exhausted, when he abandoned him, and his mother then took him up and carried him the remainder of the way.

The property left in the fort by the Kolosh was taken out, the fortification was burned and the canoes on the beach were broken to pieces. There was enough remaining of the structure that some of the remains of the foundation may yet be seen in the forest which has sprung up around it in the Indian River Park, although more than a century has since elapsed.

13

Sitka in 1805–From Lisianski's Voyage.

Then began the restoration of the post, on the present site of Sitka, and with energy and despatch the building of a new Russian settlement proceeded. Around the kekoor the native houses were removed, and along with them more than a hundred burial houses with the ashes of the bodies which had been burned. The great tribal houses, or barabaras, as they are called in the Russian accounts, were spacious, some measuring 50 feet in width and 80 feet in length.[2] In their place rose the town of New Archangel (*Novo Arkangelsk,*) and on the kekoor was built a redoubt. This was the official name and generally recognized by the Russians, but the name Sitka was early used by them. Baranof frequently used the term Sitka in his letters, and in the letter of the Minister of Finance to the Minister of Marine, from St. Petersburg, April 9, 1820, Sitka is used in several places. The name Sitka, or Sheetkah, in the Thlingit language, means, in this place, that this is the place, or the best place, implying superiority over all other places.

All winter there was cutting of logs in the forest and by the spring of 1805 there were eight substantial buildings, the space for 15 kitchen gardens had been cleared, the livestock brought on the ships

---

[2] In Wrangell, and at a few other places in Alaska may yet be seen some of these old tribal houses, built as in primitive days in most ways. The beams and planks were fashioned with an adze, and the evenness of the workmanship in hewing them is marvelous.

were thriving, and an air of prosperity pervaded the place.[3] Surveys of the harbor were made by Captain Lisianski who also made the first ascent of Mt. Edgecumbe, and who then sailed for Kronstadt, Russia, by the way of Canton, with a cargo of furs for the China trade valued at 450,000 rubles.[4]

---

[3] The livestock taken to Sitka in 1804 consisted of "Four cows, two calves, three bulls, three goats, a ewe and a ram, with many swine and fowls." (Lisianski, Voyage Round the World, p. 218.)

[4] Lisianski made the surveys and named the islands of the archipelago which had not been charted by Vancouver, of which he says: "By our survey it appears that amongst the group of islands, which in my chart I have denominated the Sitka Islands, from the inhabitants, who call themselves Sitka-hans, or Sitka people, are four principal ones, viz.: Jacobi, Crooze, Baranof, and Chichagof." (A Voyage Round the World, Lisianski, p. 235.)

CHAPTER III
PROGRESS OF THE
COLONY

The courtly Chamberlain of the Tsar, Nicholas P. Resanof, son-in-law of Shelikof who was the founder of the first Russian colony in America, came to Sitka in 1805, via Petropavlovsk, Siberia, on the "Nadeshda," one of the first Russian ships to circumnavigate the world, and was a special representative of the Russian American Company, of which organization he was one of the founders.

In his report to the Company he tells us: "The fort is on the high hill, or kekoor, on a peninsula in the gulf. On the left side of the kekoor close on the peninsula is built an immense barracks with two projecting blockhouses or towers. All the building is made from mast timber from the top to the foundation, under which is a cellar. Besides this building are two warehouses, a material magazine and two cellars, also two large sheds for storing food, and under the sheds are the quarters for the workmen. On the side opposite the fort is a shed for storing cargo, at the right side is the kitchen, bath, and quarters for the servants of the Company, clerks, etc., and on the shore are the blacksmith shops and other workshops. On the top of the kekoor is a building five sazhens[5] long and three sazhens wide, with two rooms. In one I live, and in the other there are two shipmasters. There are still some old Kolosh *yourts*, in which live the *kayours* and the Kodiak Americans (Aleuts, they are generally called).[6]

"Our guns are always loaded, everywhere are sentinels with loaded arms, and in the rooms of each of us arms constitute the greater part of the furniture. All the night the signals from post to post con-

---

[5] The Russian sazhen is 7 feet.
[6] Pronounced Al-e-ut.

tinue, war discipline prevails; in a word, we are ready at any minute to receive our dear guests, who generally profit by the darkness of night to make an attack."

The additional number in the garrison owing to the arrival of the Chamberlain and his suite made it more difficult to procure provisions for the winter. The hostile Kolosh made hunting and fishing dangerous. In the autumn there was but flour enough for an allowance of a pound a week for one month for the 200 men in the fort. For other food supply they were dependent on the fish caught in the bay, the dried *yukali* and sealion meat from Kodiak, and the dried seal meat from the Seal Islands.

Baranof bought the ship "Juno," an American sailing ship of about 250 tons, from Captain George D'Wolf, of Bristol, Conn., with its cargo of flour, sugar and other articles, for the sum of 68,000 piastres (Spanish), equivalent to about the same number of dollars. This relieved the immediate necessity, but before spring the supply became so low that the scurvy, that dread malady of the seas and of outlying localities, attacked the garrison. This scourge often fell heavily on the early Russian expeditions, and in 1821 the Russian ship "Borodino" lost 40 men through its ravages in a voyage from Sitka to Kronstadt.

In March, Resanof sailed for San Francisco in the "Juno" to purchase breadstuffs and other supplies. He also wished to examine the coast with the view of making other settlements farther south, at Nootka, at the Columbia, or even farther south in California. He secured a cargo of the products of the south and returned to Sitka in June.

On his southward journey Resanof reconnoitred the mouth of the Columbia River, seeking a site for a future settlement. He was unable to enter the river owing to contrary winds; and the condition of his crew, debilitated by lack of proper food and suffering from scurvy, caused him to hasten on. He heard that a party of U. S. soldiers were building a fort there. This rumor doubtless came from the presence of Lewis and Clarke near the present Astoria.

While on this visit to San Francisco Resanof met the Spanish beauty, Dona Concepcion de Arguello, of whom one of the visitors said, "She was lively and animated, had sparkling, love-inspiring eyes, beautiful teeth, pleasing and expressive features, a fine form and a thousand other charms," and he lost his heart to her. The romance of the Russian courtier and the fair Californian furnished to Bret Harte the theme for some of his most beautiful verse. Resanof, hurrying home to Russia to gain the Imperial permission to his marriage, died at

Krasnoyarsk, Siberia, and Dona Concepcion waited for years for the coming of her lover, not knowing that he lay dead under the Siberian snows. When the news of his sad fate came to her she donned the habit of a nun and devoted herself to charitable works.

This visit to California was the beginning of a trade that continued for many years, through all the period of Russian occupation. During the days of the gold discoveries in California large shipments of goods were made from Sitka to San Francisco, and after the sale of the territory to the United States great quantities of merchandise were shipped from the warehouses of the Company to the California metropolis, amounting to over a quarter of a million dollars in one year.

The breadstuffs for the colonies were procured from California, from San Francisco and from Ross Colony, or from Peru, until 1840, when a contract was made with the Hudson's Bay Company under which the supplies were brought from the farms of the Nisqually or from Vancouver, in Oregon Territory.

Until the time of the arrival of the "Neva", 1804, all trading goods were brought across Siberia to Okhotsk, and thence by sailing vessel to the colony, or were purchased from the American or English trading ships which came to the coast for furs. To the natives the English who came to these waters became known as "King George Men," and the Americans were called "Boston Men," the latter being from the great number of ships that sailed from the great shipping port of New England. From these traders goods were purchased by Baranof at lower rates than those cost which were brought from Russia. John Jacob Astor was one of the first to engage in the trade. He sent the ship "Enterprise" to Sitka in 1810, and the "Beaver" in 1812. From Washington Irving we have the description, through the account of the Captain, of the "Hyperborean veteran ensconsed in a fort which crested the top of a high rock promontory," which is well known to all readers of stories of western life, and in which the impression of the character of Baranof as given to the reader is very erroneous. The traders exchanged their goods with the Russians for furs, sometimes going to the Pribilof Islands to receive the seal-skins; sailed to China, where the furs were traded for silks, nankins, and teas; they then voyaged on around the world to their home port.

The sloop-of-war "Diana," the first Russian warship to reach Sitka, arrived in 1810 under the command of Captain Vasili M. Golofnin, who was widely known for his adventures while a captive in the Kingdom of the Nipponese, where he was carried about in a bamboo cage and exhibited to the populace. His description of his visit to Sitka is entertaining, and of it he says:

"In the fort we met nothing so unusual or costly as to be worthy of special remark; the fort consisted of solid log towers, and high strong palisades, with apertures or embrasures, in which were set guns and carronades of different calibres. The interior construction, barracks, storehouses, house of the commander and other buildings were made of thick logs and were very solid, these being very common in this place, around which grows, so to say, within reach of a windlass, a multitude of most beautiful trees suitable for structures of every description.

"In the house of Mr. Baranof were ornaments and furniture in profusion, of masterly workmanship and costly price, brought from St. Petersburg and from England, which corresponded with his position as the head official of a great company. What astonished us most was an extensive library in nearly all European languages, and many pictures of remarkable merit. I must confess, that I badly judge in painting, and only could know, that in the uncultivated wild border of America, there would be none except Mr. Baranof to value and understand them, unless there might happen to be educated travelers, or masters of United States trading vessels visiting this place, there would be no one to appreciate the fine art. Mr. Baranof, noting my astonishment, explained the riddle, saying, that the pictures attracting our attention were gifts of the Company and of distinguished persons in St. Petersburg, for the establishing of a library, and the Directory sent them out. On these works he commented with the following remarkable view: 'Better that our directors had sent us a doctor, for in all the Company's colonies there is not one doctor, nor one doctor's assistant, nor one doctor's pupil.'"

Golofnin soon left Sitka to return to St. Petersburg. His successful voyage, together with that of the "Neva" and the "Nadeshda," encouraged the shipment of goods by sea from Russia, and from that time onward ships came regularly, laden with supplies of every kind for the post, and returned with rich cargoes of peltry.

By 1825 surgical and astronomical instruments of the best quality were sent to the colony, an apothecary shop of three rooms provided medicines, and four Creole boys, under the charge of a doctor, attended to the dispensing of the potions. A hospital was in connection and the sick received fresh food, tea, sugar, and medicines, free, upon the order of the doctor.

An observatory, equipped with the most improved magnetic and meteorological instruments was later provided and there was kept a record of natural phenomena, while a museum of objects of interest from the surrounding country was open for the instruction of all.

The library was brought from St. Petersburg in 1806 by Resanof. Mr. Khlebnikof tells us that it contained more than 1,200 volumes, valued at 7,500 rubles, and they were in the Russian, French, German, English, Latin and other languages.

When Mr. Resanof was preparing for his journey he addressed letters to many of the leading men of St. Petersburg, soliciting their contribution of books to promote the beginning of education in the far off possession of the Czar. Many sent a response in writing accompanied by one or more volumes, and the letters so sent were richly bound in a separate volume and placed with the library in the building at Sitka. Among the patrons were the Metropolite Ambrosia, Count Rumiantzof, Count Stroganof, Admiral Chichagof, Minister of Justice Dimitrief, Senator Zakarof and others. The sentiments were varied, but many agreed in voicing the desire to "sow the seed of science in the breasts of the peoples so far outlying from the enlightenment of Europe." Some of them reflected the personal character of the donors: The Metropolite Ambrosia sent books for church services; the Minister of Marine sent plans of ships; and Count Rumiantzof contributed works on husbandry.[7]

Mr. Kyril Khlebnikof, the accountant of the Company, who was in charge of the counting house at Sitka from 1818 to 1832, to whom we are indebted for many valuable writings relating to the early history of the settlements, tells us that when Mr. Baranof left the colony the buildings had become badly decayed and much new construction had to be done. In 1827 there had been built, three sentry houses, a battery of thirty guns on the kekoor, and below them magazines, barracks and other buildings, a bakery, wharf, arsenal, etc. In the shops were blacksmiths, coppersmiths, locksmiths, coopers, turners, rope spinners, chandlers, painters, masons, etc.

---

[7] These books and letters were brought by Resanof in the "Nedeshda," and upon reaching Kodiak Resanof established the library at that place. It was afterward removed to Sitka, probably by Baranof when he changed the chief factory to that place in 1807. After the United States took possession the library disappeared, whether taken to Russia or left in Sitka does not appear, but the books were likely left in Sitka and gradually disappeared through theft in the years when there was no custodian of such property.

At the Ozerskoe Redoubt, on Deep Lake, were barracks and a fort, a flouring mill, a tannery, and other buildings. A zapor, or fish trap, in the stream took sixty thousand fish each year.

The Bakery and Shops of the Russians–Later the Sitka Trading Co.'s Building.

The workmen got out timber from the forest for the building of ships, they cut fuel and burned charcoal in large quantities; kept the buildings in repair and did other duties required on the factory. The work of the gardening was chiefly done by the Aleuts, who were paid a ruble a day for their services.

The Russian Captain Lutke came to Sitka about this time and he tells us that there were many pigs and chickens raised by the inhabitants, and that a pig might be had for 5 to 7 rubles, a hen for 4 to 5 rubles, and eggs at from 3-1/2 to 10 rubles per dozen. The chief drawback to the chicken industry was the presence of the great black ravens that carried away the young chicks and sometimes even the old hens. The ravens were such successful scavengers that they were called the New Archangel police, and he says they even bit the tails off the young pigs, so that all the hogs of the place were tailless.

He mentions the abundance of deer on the islands and also says that mountain sheep were killed by the Aleuts and brought to the fort. He must have confused the sheep with the goats, for the sheep never approach the coast so closely, and he speaks of the wool being used for weaving the blankets for the ceremonial dances of the Kolosh.

21

This would indicate that the animal in question was the mountain goat. A later writer says that 2,700 game animals were brought into Sitka for sale during the winter of 1861-62.

A shipyard was established as soon as the necessary buildings to house the garrison were completed. It occupied a part of the present parade ground near the Russian Barracks and included a portion of the present street. Many vessels were built in the yard during the Russian occupation, the first, being the tender "Avoss," launched in 1806, followed by the brig "Sitka," built by an American shipbuilder named Lincoln, and for which he was paid 2,000 rubles as a royalty upon the completion of the ship. A frigate of 320 tons was the largest vessel built before 1819, and at that time construction was discontinued until 1834, when work was resumed and continued until the close of the Russian regime.

The "Politofsky" was one of the last vessels to be built at Sitka, and it was sold by Prince Maksoutoff to H. M. Hutchinson and Abraham Hirsch for $4,000 in 1867. The next year it was sold to Hutchinson, Kohl & Co., and later was sold to a firm that ran it to Puget Sound, and from Alaska to San Francisco. It was built of Alaska cedar timber, the *dushnoi dereva* or scented wood of the Russians, and was spiked with hand-made copper spikes. It was taken to Alaska in the gold rush of 1898, and found its last resting place, very appropriately, in the land where it was built, in the harbor of St. Michael, the old Russian port on Bering Sea.

The fear of shipwreck, and of death at sea hung over every soul of the community. The long voyages in uncharted and unlighted waters with sailing ships—more than six months at the shortest from Kronstadt—often three months or more against baffling winds from Okhotsk—the voyages to the redoubts and *odinoshkas* (detached posts with one man only) of the Bering Sea and of the Gulf of Alaska, to collect the fur catch of the year and bring it to Sitka; the long journey via Canton on the return to Russia—all held many dangers for the sailing ships of those days. The "Phoenix," the first ship built on the Alaskan shores, foundered with all on board, including the Bishop and his retinue, in 1799, on the return voyage from Okhotsk; the "St. Nicholas" went ashore on the coast of Washington in 1808, and those who survived the waves were held in bondage for years by the savages of that coast.

During the latter part of August, 1812, the ship "Neva" left Okhotsk—contrary winds delayed her in the Sea of Okhotsk—storms beat her back along the Aleutian Islands till it was November before land was sighted in Alaska. The storms damaged the rigging and ship until it was necessary to put into Voskresenski Harbor (Resurrection Bay) for repairs. She arrived off Sitka about December 1st. After four or five days Mt. Edgecumbe was sighted but a storm drove the ship to sea where she beat about for weeks before again nearing the port. Scurvy afflicted the passengers and crew and added to the general distress. On January 8th, 1813, Mt. Edgecumbe again appeared. In trying to make the harbor the ship grounded on the rocks under the cape on the morning of the 9th and speedily broke to pieces under the terrific pounding of the seas.[8] Some of the people on board reached shore after incredible suffering and hardship.

After several days two of the sailors wandering along the shore met a Kolosh boy and persuaded him to take them to Sitka, where they arrived, cold, exhausted, and almost starving. Boats were at once fitted out by Mr. Baranof, the survivors were rescued, brought to Sitka, and their sufferings relieved. From those on board the ship, 38 had perished, including Kalinin, the commander, Boronovolokof, the intended future chief manager of the Company, and five women passengers. In the cargo was food and clothing, the messages of the year for the exiles, and rich vestments and furnishings for the church that was soon to be built in Sitka, all scattered for miles along the wild coast of Kruzof Island. This was one of the worst disasters of the sea that visited the colony, although many others are part of the records of the time.

It is said that Chief Katlean tore his hair with rage when he learned of the wreck, because he did not find it and destroy the survivors out of revenge for his defeat and expulsion from his home at Sitka.

There are many traditions among the residents of Sitka concerning the wreck of the "Neva." Among them is that there was a vast treasure of gold for the use of the garrison and the traders. This is erroneous, for there was no gold used in the colonies, the trade being by barter or conducted with scrip, called *assignats*, issued by the Company for the purpose. The story of the gold has been so generally

---

[8] The "Neva" was long identified with the affairs of the colony. Bought in England for the first Russian expedition round the world, Captain Lisianski reached Sitka in time for her to participate in the driving of the Indians from their fortifications. She returned to Russia later to be sailed to the colony in 1810, and was on her third voyage at the time of her loss.

believed that serious plans have been made for attempting the salvage of the treasure.

The term of office of Alexander Andreevich Baranof as the chief manager of the Russian American Company came to a close in 1818. He had been 28 years in the colonies, leaving Russia in 1790 for the post of Three Saints on Kodiak Island, which at that time constituted almost the only Russian establishment in America, the other stations being little more than outlying trading posts. He left their dominion an empire in extent, reaching from the Seal Islands in Bering Sea, at the edge of the ice pack of the Arctic, to Fort Ross, among the sunny hills of Golden California. Captain Hagmeister came to relieve him, and in his 72nd year the old chief manager, bent with the weight of years and of long and arduous service, closed his accounts and set sail on the "Kutusof," one of the Company's vessels, for his far-off home in Russia.

When the time arrived for Baranof to take his departure from the land he had made his home for so many years, sorrowfully he took his leave of the associates with whom he had so long shared the dangers and hardships of the uncivilized land. Upon being relieved of the duties of his office he first considered building a home at the Ozerskoe Redoubt and spending the remainder of his days in the place he had learned to love. Later he decided to return to his native land and sailed on the "Kutusof" for Kronstadt. A delay at Batavia in the tropics proved too severe for his advanced years. The day after leaving Batavia he died and was buried at sea in the waters of the Indian Ocean.

Captain Leontius Andreanovich Hagemeister succeeded to the office of chief manager but remained only a short time at Sitka, then sailed for Russia, leaving Captain Simeon Ivanovich Yanovski in charge.

Captain Yanovski became enamored with the beautiful daughter of Baranof, and if you search the old records of the Cathedral of St. Michaels at Sitka you will find the entry as made of the marriage of Simeon Ivanof Yanovski "with the late head governor of the Russian American possessions, Collegiate Adviser and Cavalier Baranof's daughter Irina, one of Creoles."

In 1830, Baron Ferdinand Petrovich Wrangell, scientist and explorer, came to administer the office. He had sailed the frozen ocean along the northern shores of Siberia as an explorer, and Wrangell Island, Wrangell Strait, etc., on the maps of today perpetuate his name.

Under Baron Wrangell, as assistant to the manager, served Adolph Carlovich Etolin, a native of Finland, who came to the colony as an officer on the war sloop "Kamchatka" in 1817, who sailed in the service of the Company to nearly every port from the Seal Islands of Bering Sea to Chile, who made several voyages around the world, and who was made chief manager in 1840. In 1846 he returned to Russia to accept the trust of Commercial Counsellor in the head office of the Company in St. Petersburg.

About fourteen miles to the southwest, across the bay and facing Edgecumbe, with a beautiful view of the peak and islands, is the Hot Springs, well known for their medicinal properties by the natives before the advent of the Russians, and frequently resorted to by both as a panacea for many ills. In the Place of Islands *(Chasti Ostrova)* is reputed to be a spring with a sour taste, while almost within the limits of the town of Sitka, Dr. Scheffer, a German physician who made a sojourn in the place about 1815, claimed to have found a medical spring whose waters were equal to some of the famed watering places of Germany.

CHAPTER IV
NATIVES

Most of the Sitkan Kolosh kept aloof from the Russian settlement after the establishment of the new fort on Chatham Strait, near the entrance of Peril Strait. All the kwans, the Khootznoos, the Hoonahs, the Chilkats, the Auks, Stikines, Kakes and others, joined with the Sitkas in the hatred of the Russians. Parties going out from the fort at Sitka for hunting expeditions, for cutting of wood, for traveling to the Hot Springs, had to be on their guard and with arms at hand prepared to fight at a moment's notice.[9] Small groups were often cut off and murdered. As it was impossible to decide which of the many kwans did the act, and as there were those in each kwan who were peaceable, with whom it was desired to keep the peace, revenge against any village was inadvisable. Even as late as the date of the lease to the Hudson's Bay Co. the Russian ships that sailed among the islands to trade with the Kolosh were compelled to act with the strictest caution. Only a few natives were admitted on board at a time, the trading was done in a space near the stern, and was conducted under the muzzles of loaded cannon concealed in the fore part of the ship.[10] The conditions were thus until 1821, when the Sitkas were invited to reoccupy the site of the old village and to live in what is now known as the "Ranche," under the guns of the redoubt.

The Thlingit nation is a strange, warlike, shrewd people, physically strong and enduring, and possessed of many excellent qualities. Hunters and fishermen by nature and training, they are skillful boatmen, and in those days they built wonderfully beautiful canoes of the red cedar, some of them large enough to carry sixty men at the paddles. Each spring more than a thousand men gathered together in

---

[9] Golofnin, Voyage of the Sloop "Kamchatka," in Mat. Pt. 4, p. 103.
[10] Lutke: Voyages. Mat. Pt. 4, p. 147

Sitka Bay, coming from the different villages, to fish for herring at the spawning time, when those fish run in countless myriads in those waters. Hemlock boughs were placed in the water, and on them the herring roe collected until they were encrusted with the eggs which were then stripped off and dried for future use.

The "Ranche"–Looking north from the top of the Baranof Castle, the Steamer at the left is the "Coquitlam," noted for her participation in pelagic sealing and she was under seizure by the U. S. Government.

In 1807 there were over 2,000 hostile natives gathered in the harbor at the herring season and they threatened an attack on the settlement. Kuskof, the most trusted and able lieutenant of Baranof, was in charge, and it put his wisdom and watchfulness to the test to avert disaster. The strictest discipline was maintained. The tribesmen waited outside day after day, hoping for news of some relaxation of the precautions of the defenders to be brought to them by the women of the tribe who were married to the Russian promishleniki (hunters). Day and night the sentinels paced the beats on the stockade and along the waterfront, till, weary of waiting, the Kolosh finally dispersed to their homes.

In the great tribal houses several families lived, sometimes as many as fifty or sixty persons. Over the door of the house was painted the family totem, for the Sitkas did not raise the house totem in a pole in front as did many of the kwans of the Thlingits, and as the Hydahs do. In these houses were held the potlatches, or gift parties, which were made by the wealthy chiefs.

The potlatches were of different kinds, although all partook of the nature of a feasting or merrymaking and were distinguished by the giving of gifts. In the ordinary visiting potlatches, or in the berry potlatches, the visitors came in their canoes with which they formed a line off shore opposite the houses, put planks from one canoe to another and on these planks danced the tribal dance. Those on shore danced the welcome dance and invited the guests ashore. Then the visitors disembarked and each family became the guest of their kinsmen of their totem or they went to the guesthouse of the kwan. All the people of the same totem are supposed to be blood relations, so all those of the wolf totem go to the *Gooch-heat*, or the dwelling blazoned by the rude heraldry with the wolf rampant. In the great social potlatches a wealthy chief invites his friends from many villages and entertains them for a week or more with dancing and feasting and makes presents varied and valuable, from Hudson's Bay blankets to bolts of calico or of flannel, and in primitive days, copper tows,[11] Chilkat blankets, and even slaves were handed over with a lavish hospitality.

On special occasions in the olden time, with great ceremony the visitors landed at a distance from the village, drew their canoes ashore and proceeded to the village dressed in festive garments adorned with sealion heads or other strange headdresses, in which they danced the rare and picturesque "Beach Dance," in acknowledgement to the Spirit of the Sea for the bountiful supply of salmon and herring of the past season–for the native American is a thankful being and omits not to show it when occasion offers to acknowledge it to the Giver of all good and perfect gifts.

During the earlier years of the colony the Kolosh were implacable enemies. War parties of young men constantly haunted the islands of the bay, lying in wait for any unwary hunter or fisherman from the fort. Later, when they were settled under the walls of the fort they became more tractable, for their homes and families were commanded by the guns of the fortress, but on the least provocation the savagery in their blood would boil, from their great tribal houses they issued forth, faces blackened to the semblance of devils, war masks grinning, and the howling mob shouted defiance at their neighbor over the stockade. Many a bloody tragedy was enacted in the "Ranche" for their code was primitive, "an eye for an eye," and a life for a life.

---

[11] The tows were large pieces of native copper from the Copper River hammered out flat by the natives. These were carried in front of the chiefs by slaves who beat them like gongs.

28

Feuds raged between the different totemic families. About 1853 a party of Wrangell Indians (Stikines) visited Sitka, and while being entertained in the guest-house were murdered and their bodies piled into a canoe which was then paddled to Japonski Island. On striking the shore it was so heavily laden with the bodies of the dead that tradition says the canoe split from end to end. It is said that the bones of the dead are still to be seen in the undergrowth along the shore. In retaliation, about 1855, the Wrangell Kolosh made an attack on the Hot Springs settlement, burned the buildings, stripped the inhabitants of property and clothing and left them to make their way over the mountains around the head of Silver Bay to Sitka, where they arrived more dead than alive from hunger and exhaustion. This feud was not settled until 1918, when a peace treaty was consummated between the kwans on Armistice Day, a coincidence which is much made of by the tribesmen.

The Kolosh were as firm believers in witchcraft as any of the more civilized nations. They resorted to their shamans (*ekhts*) or medicine men in case of illness. If his weird incantations failed to relieve the sufferer, his resort was that the victim was bewitched and some poor unfortunate paid the penalty by enduring the most fiendish torture.

One March day in 1855 a commotion arose in the Kolosh village. A sentry caught an Indian who was stealing and punished him, for which the tribe called for vengeance. Some rushed to the stockade and began to cut away the palisades. Other forced their way into the Koloshian Church through the outer door. From this vantage point they fired on the garrison and in return the batteries of the fort blazed back with solid shot and shrapnel. For two hours the fight continued, when the Kolosh gave up all hope of success, and ceased the battle. The Russian loss in killed and wounded was 20 men, while the Kolosh loss was estimated at 60. This was the last attempt of the natives to destroy the Russian stronghold.

At times during the later days of the colony the Kolosh were employed as seamen and as workers in the ice trade by the Russians and thus they occupied a place in the industrial life. Etolin was the most successful in conciliating them of any of the chief managers, and he at one time held a fur fair at Sitka to which peltry was brought from far and near, modeled somewhat upon the idea of the great fur mart of Nizhni Novgorod. Most of them, however, hunted and fished, lived in their tribal houses, carved their canoes, wove their baskets, and practiced their witchcraft, while their civilized neighbors gathered the furs and built ships.

Under the walls of the fort, in the old tribal houses of the Kolosh which had not been destroyed, lived the Aleuts. Properly speaking the name belongs to the natives of the Aleutian Islands, but the term was also applied to the natives of Kodiak Island and the surrounding islets. These speak a different language from the true Aleuts, but otherwise resemble them closely. During the hunting season they scoured the seas in their skin bidarkas, in the pursuit of fur animals. In winter many of them remained at Sitka instead of returning to their homes. Their time was spent in idleness, spending the summer's earnings in the pleasures and vices of the white man. One who saw them in their kazhims, as their dwellings were often called, describes them: "Morally, the Aleut is not bloodthirsty. He delights in simple rejoicings and will play you a game of chess with walrus ivory pieces–a duck for a pawn and a penguin for a king–with the greatest of good humor. Even when squabbles arrive the argument is carried on in poetry to the accompaniment of dancing, and one would be inclined to prefer the Aleut angry to the Aleut amiable, did he not know he also dances when festive and when religious.

"Among them the social duty of visiting has its drawbacks. Several families live together in the kazhims, and during one's visit they all lie around in every conceivable posture, jolly and genial, naked and unashamed. The fumes of the blubber oil lamps and stoves, the stores of raw meat, the many naked bodies, well smeared with grease and scented with primitive unguents, combine to make an atmosphere difficult to tolerate and not easy to describe. Yet, if you will, you may enjoy the warmest hospitality, and have heaped upon you the most assiduous attentions."

CHAPTER V
CHURCHES AND
SCHOOLS

It was not until 1816 that a priest arrived at Sitka, and in that year the first entry is made in the church records under the name of Alexander Sokolof. A church was built at the south of the street, which was then called the Governor's Walk, almost opposite the present cathedral. A monument marks the spot where the altar stood, and a cross marks the site of a grave, said to be that of a priest. Tradition also tells that there are two graves there, and assigns the other one to the daughter of Baron Wrangell, the chief manager of the Company at one time.[12]

The present cathedral of St. Michael, which is the central point of historic interest, in the center of the town at Lincoln Street, was dedicated November 20, 1848. It fronts on a small court and with its green painted spire surmounted by the Greek Cross is so typically Russian that it might readily be believed to have been transplanted from old Russia. The chime of bells, a gift from the Church at Moscow, would be worthy of any shrine. The building is in the form of a cross, has three sanctuaries and three altars. The larger and central sanctuary is that of the *Archistrategos* Michael. In the center is an elevated platform, the episcopal *Cathedra*, and it is separated from the main body of the church by a partition called the *Ikonastas*, which is ornamented with twelve *ikons*, or holy paintings, covered by plates of silver in *repousse* work in the true Russian style of art, and through the

---

[12] In the church records appears the entry: "Died, August 27, 1832, Naval Captain of the 1st Rank and Cavalier Baron Ferdinand Wrangell's daughter– Mary." There is also to be found: "Died, December 29th, 1839, Priest Vasili Michaeloff Ocheredin, 23 years old."

Royal Gates the priest appears. The silver in the ikons is valued at over $6,000. The ikon of St. Michael is said to have been in the wreck of the "Neva," and was rescued after being cast up by the sea. Another is a gift of the monks of the monastery of Solovetsk; another was brought by Bishop Innocentius (Veniaminof) from Petropavlovsk. The ikon of the Resurrection is painted on a board from a tree in Hebron, was consecrated in Bethlehem, and bears the autograph signature of the Patriarch of Jerusalem.

Cathedral of St. Michael

The chapel at the right is dedicated in the name of St. John the Precursor and Prince Alexander Nevsky.

The chapel at the left is in honor of Our Lady of Kazan. In it is a painting of a Madonna and Child from which the beautiful Byzantine face looks down with a sweet radiance.

The vestments and sacred vessels are rich and elegant. The white Easter vestment is of cloth of silver and the cloth of gold for high feast days was the personal gift of Alexander Andreevich Baranof, the great Russian who established the colony. The belfry clock is said to be the work of the hands of Veniaminof. The priest in richly brocaded vestments holds the services, and a choir of boys chant the chorus with a melody that would be the envy of many a far more pretentious edifice. The worshipers stand during the services, the clouds of incense rise toward the rounded dome, then one by one the worshipers pass and kiss the jeweled cross in the hand of the priest. Father Metropolski presided over the church for many years, and Father Sergius is one of the best known in recent years.

There were two other churches during Russian days, one, a Lutheran, built during Etolin's time, which stood near the site of the first church, and is said to have contained a small but very excellent pipe organ, brought from Germany. The other church stood near the blockhouse on the hill, was on the line of the stockade, and had two doors, one inside the fortification, the other outside and used as an entrance by the natives. It was known as the Koloshian Church, and its site is marked by a monument. Both these buildings long ago fell into ruin and were removed.

The Russian religion was closely associated with the Government, so in the colonies the official charter of the Company compelled them to provide well for the church and the priests according to the standard of the times, and the work was carried on with zeal and fortitude by the missionaries who came from the monasteries of the old Russian cities.

Of all the missionaries who came to Russian America, the greatest was Ivan Veniaminof. Father John he is often called in the old records, a wonderful man, broad of mind and of body, combining the qualities that inspire awe and reverence with a gentleness of word and deed that made him beloved wherever he was known. His zapiski, or letters, are among the best authorities extant which remain from those years on Alaskan matters, and they were written home to Russia during his stay in the Aleutian Islands and at Sitka. He came to Sitka after a ten-year stay at Unalaska, remained there for five years working for the church and teaching in the schools, then returned to Moscow and was consecrated as bishop of the new diocese. He again arrived in Sitka in 1842, and made a tour of all the churches in the colonies, traveling by sailing ship to every settlement, then went home to Russia where he became Metropolite of Moscow.

The Madonna.

The schools of Sitka, under the Russian regime, were well maintained, and many of the mechanics, clerks, pilots, and men of other trades were educated there. Kadin, who drew the charts for Tebenkof's Atlas of Alaska from the surveys made by the Russian Navigators; Tarantief, who engraved the maps on copper-plate at Sitka; and many of the shipmasters and accountants in the employ of the Company, were the product of the educational institutions of Sitka. In the time of the greatest prosperity there were five schools. The church school was advanced to the grade of a seminary in 1849 and there were taught navigation, mathematics, astronomy, bookkeeping, and other branches of learning. Some of the best pupils, both Russian and Creole, were sent to St. Petersburg for more advanced instruction. Chief Manager Etolin was the especial patron of education, and made many improvements in the system. Under the auspices of Madame

Etolin, who was a native of Helsingfors and was educated in the schools of that city, a school was opened and maintained by the Company for the girls of the colony. After the transfer to the United States of the Territory the teachers returned to Russia and the schools were closed.

CHAPTER VI
SOCIAL LIFE

At the top of the kekoor, or the Baranof Hill as it was called in recent years, there stood a building occupied during Russian days as a residence by the chief managers of the Russian American Company. The one known to the residents and visitors of the earlier days of the American occupation was known as the Baranof Castle, although Baranof himself never lived in it. There were three, if not four different buildings which occupied that position. The first to be placed there was built at once upon the founding of the post and is described by Resanof in his letters to the Company as being a very "Unpretentious building, and poorly constructed." Before the close of Baranof's administration, however, according to the account of Captain Golofnin, it was an establishment well built and furnished with some degree of luxury.

The structure known as the Baranof Castle, which stood on the hill at the time of the transfer to the United States, would seem to be the third building constructed on the site, was completed about 1837,[13] and was burned to the ground on the morning of March 17th, 1894.

The historic building was the scene of many interesting events, and sheltered many distinguished persons.

The first mistress who presided over the mansion on the kekoor was Madame Yanovski, a daughter of Baranof and the wife of Lieutenant Yanovski, the third chief manager of the Russian American Company.

---

[13] Narrative of a Voyage Round the World, 1836-1842, by Captain Sir Edward Belcher, Vol. 1, pages 95 et seq.

The Baranof Castle.
Built in 1837 for the official residence of the chief managers of the
Russian American Company, and occupied from the time of Kuprianof
until 1867. It was the headquarters building of the Commanding Offi-
cers of the U. S. troops 1867 to 1877, and was destroyed by fire in
1894. The U. S. Agricultural Department building occupies the site at
the present time.

Lady Wrangell was the first to come from Russia to preside as the First Lady of Sitka, and she was succeeded by Madame Kupreanof, who is said to have crossed Siberia and the Pacific Ocean to accompany her husband to his post. Sir Edward Belcher gives a spirited account of a ball given in his honor, in the castle, which was then, in 1837, just completed. He says: "The evening passed most delight-fully," although "few could converse with their partners," English being spoken by few at that time in the capital of Russian America.

Princess Maksoutoff, the wife of the last chief manager of the colonies, came from St. Petersburg, but died soon after her arrival, and the stone which marks her grave may be seen on the hill between the two cemeteries, near the site of the upper Blockhouse. Her successor, the second Princess Maksoutoff, young and beautiful, presided with grace and tact over the mansion until the transfer of the territory to the United States. She was one of six Russian ladies present at the ceremonies and is said to have wept when the Russian flag was lowered.

There is a legend of a beautiful princess whose ghost haunted the Castle for many years. The story has been told by many at different times and is one of the romantic tales that cluster around the old metropolis of the fur trading days. Her lover was sent away or killed through the influence of an *ober offitzer* who sought her hand in mar-

37

riage. Eliza Ruhamah Scidmore, who wrote so delightfully of Sitka in her journeys in Alaska in 1883, says that, "By tradition the Lady in Black was the daughter of one of the old governors. On her wedding night she disappeared from the ballroom in the midst of the festivities, and after a long search was found dead in one of the small drawing rooms."[14]

The chief managers entertained lavishly, and the dinners in the Castle were events long to be remembered. They were well worthy the representatives of a rich and powerful company, a corporation with a domain that was greater than the realm of many a royal ruler. Into the sumptuously furnished and richly decorated dining-room came the bishop and priests, resplendent in the official robes, the naval officers glittering in their gold laced uniforms, the secretaries, accountants, storekeepers, all in the uniform of the Ministry of Finance, the masters and mates of the ships in the harbor; the guests in their best apparel; all gathered around the hospitable board of the chief manager. At times a hundred sat at the table and back of them dined the cadets of the naval school. After the dinner came dancing and until morning the gayety went merrily on, for Russian cheer is proverbial, and their hospitality is lavish.

Usually the Captain of the port, the secretaries, three public and two private, two masters in the navy, the commercial agent, two doctors, and the Lutheran clergyman, dined with the chief manager by general invitation, Sir George Simpson tells us. The civilian masters of vessels, accountants, engineers, clerks, and bookkeepers, dined at a club which was organized by Mr. Etolin, and they lived at the old club house a little to the east of the church.

---

[14] Frederick Schwatka, the explorer, seems to have been one of the first to put the story in print, which he did in the early eighties. It appeared in the Alaska News, a newspaper of Juneau, on December 24th, 1896, and the time is fixed as being in the administration of Baron Wrangell. In 1891 Hon. Henry E. Hayden published it in verse in a small volume printed at Sitka. John W. Arctander, in his Lady in Blue, elaborates it to a small volume and ascribes it to Etolin's time.

There is a strange fact which gives some color to the story. In the Russian American Company's Archives now on file in the State Department, Washington, D. C., under date of September 23rd, 1833, a letter from St. Petersburg refers to a report of Baron Wrangell of November 30, 1831, which reported the death of under officer Paul Buikof, and implicating one Col. Borusof. Unfortunately the records of 1831 are missing and so the report cannot be had. Baron Wrangell's daughter, Mary, died during his stay in Sitka

The Grave of the Princess Maksoutoff.

A wedding was an elaborate affair, a bridal cake which figured in many mystic signs, tea, coffee, chocolate and champagne; the ladies attired in muslin dresses, white satin shoes, silk stockings, kid gloves, fans, and other necessary appurtances. After the ceremony of an hour and a half was consummated, the ball was opened by the bride and the highest officer present, and the dancing lasted until three in the morning.

Easter was an event of much hilarity after the close of Lent, which was strictly observed by all. From morning to night everyone ran a gauntlet of kisses; when two persons met, one said, "Christ has risen," while the other replied, "He has risen, indeed," and then followed the salutations. These seemed not to have been distasteful to visitors, although one remarks that most of the dames had been more liberal with other liquids than of pure water. Throughout it all was a continuous peal of bells, for the Russian is fond of bell-ringing. All carried eggs, boiled into stones, and dyed, gilded or painted, which they presented to their friends.

CHAPTER VII
TRADE AND INDUSTRY

Sitka, under the Muscovite, existed because of the fur trade, and every energy and interest centered on the gathering of peltries from every available quarter. Sailing ships moved in and out of the harbor, taken to their moorings or out to sea by the harbor tug; some from Michaelovsk with the beaver and martin from the Yukon, others *en route* to California or to the Sandwich Islands; the supply ships from Kronstadt around Cape Horn or returning via Canton and the Cape of Good Hope laden with furs; still others bound for the Kuril Islands or Okhotsk. The steamer "Nikolai" plied along the passages of the Alexander Archipelago, exploring the inlets, surveying the bays and rivers, gathering furs, always furs, for that was the reason for their living on this distant shore.[15]

Near the entrance to the Kolosh village was the market where the natives were permitted to trade. There they brought their game and fish, their furs and baskets, to trade for calico and beads, blankets and ammunition.[16] This market was closed by a portcullised door which permitted entrance through the stockaded wall, and was enclosed by a railed yard. Armed guards stood on duty, and at the least dispute in the market, down came the door and they proceeded to punish the delinquents.

---

[15] Between 1821 and 1862 there were shipped by the Russian American Company, from Alaska, 51,315 sea-otter, 831,396 fur-seal, 319,514 beaver, 291,655 fox. Fur-Seal Arbitration, Vol. 2, p. 127 (Washington, Government Printing Office).

[16] "For the largest deer, which weighs about four poods, five sazhens of calico are paid; for a duck, a quid of tobacco; for a goose, two quids; fish priced according to size all according to price list established by the commander of the post of New Archangel." Russkie na Vostochnom Okean (Russians on the Eastern Ocean), by A. Markof, St. Petersburg, 1856.

Sitka in 1860, Near the Close of the Russian Administration.

The warehouses were stored with thousands on thousands of the richest furs of the Northland; sea-otter, worth today from $800 to $1,000 per skin, and not to be had at any price, were numbered by thousands in the earlier years; sealskins by shiploads, some killed off the harbor, but mainly from the Seal Islands; of land otter, the Hudson's Bay Company paid them two thousand skins each year for the lease of the territory from Portland Canal to Cape Spencer. The martin, the American sable, with its fluffy pelage. Foxes, blue, white, black, silver gray, red and cross, were there by thousands, brought from the Arctic, from the Aleutian Islands, from the Valley of the Yukon; mink, ermine, muskrat, beaver, land otter, pile on pile. Tons of ivory from the walrus herds of Morzhovia and bearskins and wolfskins from Cook Inlet and the Copper River. The right to the fur trade belonged exclusively to the Company by Royal ukase, and any employe who was found attempting to infringe on their rights was arrested and sent to Russia for punishment.[17]

From the top of the Castle, over 100 feet above the sea, a light burned as a beacon to mariners entering the harbor, and this was the first light-house to throw its beams over the waters of this northern ocean. In the cupola which rose from the roof were four little square

---

[17] Hunters who disposed of their furs to an English shipmaster were arrested and sent to Siberia. Russian American Archives. Corr. Vol. I, p. 275. In January of 1820 Muravief was ordered to watch certain officers of a ship who were suspected of trading for furs on their own account. Id. Vol. 2, p. 38.

cups into which seal oil was poured and wicks burned in grooves rising from them, while back of the flame was a reflector that threw the light far out to sea among the islands.

The stock of goods in the magazines was large and varied. It covered almost every article carried in the general European trade as a necessity, and many of the luxuries–sugar and sealing wax, tobacco, both Virginia and Kirghis, silk and broadcloth, calico and Flemish linen, ravens duck and frieze, arshins of blankets and poods of yarn; vedras of rum, cognac and gin; butter from the Yakut, from California and from Kodiak; salt beef from Ross Colony, from England and from Kodiak; beaver hats and cotton socks.

In the arsenal were kept about a thousand muskets, three hundred pistols, two hundred rifles, as well as sabres, cutlasses, etc., while four fire engines provided against loss by conflagration. Some rare weapons were also found there. A saber set with gems valued at 560 rubles; a Persian carbine of a value of 450 rubles; two Persian yatighans, silver mounted; a Damascus saber, and two Persian pistols, silver mounted.

The soldiers' guns were for a great part of French or English workmanship; rockets and false-fire for signalling ships were made each year.

Tallow for candles was brought from California, moulded at the port and distributed so many candles to each employe according to their presumed needs each month.

Liquors, generally rum, were served by the Company, a drink twice a week, extra allowance being made on difficult work and also for holidays. All kinds of devices were resorted to by individuals in order to get rum, and one author says that a pair of boots for which the makers would demand ten rubles might be secured in barter for a bottle of rum worth three rubles.

The soldiers stationed at the fort when not on duty were employed by the Company and given a special compensation for their labor. Some of the soldiers and hunters by their industry and thrift accumulated considerable money which the Company held to their account and either paid to them on their discharge or sent home to Russia for them. Others spent their earnings, were continually in debt to the Company, and as their contract provided that they were not to be discharged while in arrears of debt, some of them served the remainder of their lives with no hope of return to Russia.

Around the hill ran a parapet and sentries walked their beat night and day. On the stockade which enclosed the town from the beach at the edge of the "Ranche" to the shore beyond the sawmill, making with the shore line an irregular rectangle, also walked the sentinels on their vigil, for the Thlingit at the gates was at all times an enemy to be feared. Strict military discipline was maintained at all times. At the foot of the hill were clustered barracks, storehouses, bakeries, warehouses, etc., for the use of the garrison and workmen. The old structure which was used as a bakery, and for shops, was later known as the Sitka Trading Company's building, and has recently been removed. The barracks are at present the jail, and the Russian counting house is today the postoffice of the United States. The fur warehouse stood to the west of the hill and was torn down in 1897-8, while the landing warehouse on the wharf was burned in 1916. These were all built about the time of the incumbency of Etolin, and that time might be termed the Golden Age of the Colony. Ships were being built, the fur trade was still prosperous, new explorations were being made into the interior of the country, trade was being extended into the Yukon Valley and there was an active interest in all the industries of the settlement. There were men of many trades, engineers, cabinet makers, jewelers, tailors, builders, etc., and an efficient machine shop constructed engines to equip the vessels constructed in the shipyard. Plowshares and spades for the Spanish farmers in California were forged and bells for the Franciscan missions were cast here. The first steam vessel to be built on the shore of the North Pacific Ocean was constructed at Sitka, for, before 1840 the whole of the machinery for a tug of seven horsepower, as well as of two pleasure boats had been constructed here. The steamer "Nikolai" of 70 horsepower was built and equipped with the exception of the boilers which were brought from New York. The ship ways at Sitka was the repairing place for many a vessel in the days of the gold seekers in the valleys of California.

Two sawmills, one near the site of the present mill, the other on Kirenski River, now called Sawmill Creek,[18] cut the lumber for the settlement and for export. Two flouring mills, one in Sitka, the other at the Ozerskoe Redoubt on Globokoe[19] (Deep) Lake, ground the bread-

---

[18] The mill on Sawmill Creek was located in the gorge below where the dam is situated which provides the power for the present light plant of the town. The timbers of the old mill were removed in 1916 to make way for the building of the present improvement.

[19] Golobokoe Lake was sounded to a depth of 190 fathoms by the Russians. Materialui, Pt. 3, p. 48.

stuffs. A tannery furnished the leather for shoes, made from California hides, and also prepared the *lavtaks* for the bidarkas for the seal and sea-otter hunters. The burrs for the Sitka mill were of the finest French stone but those at the Redoubt were cut from the granite found on the lake shore.[20]

A hospital of forty beds provided for the comfort of the sick, of which Governor Simpson said: "The institution in question would do no disgrace to England."

Brickyards were maintained, ice was cut on the lakes and at times shipped to California. The ice-houses were near the outlet of Swan Lake and were of a capacity of 3,000 tons.

One day in the spring of 1852 the American ship "Bacchus" came into Sitka to purchase a cargo of ice. All the ice for San Francisco had to this time been brought in the hold of sailing ships around Cape Horn from Boston and the idea of getting the supply from Sitka was conceived. From the Company's icehouses was laden on the ship 250 tons, and this was the beginning of a trade during the year of not less than 1800 tons at an average price of about $25.00 per ton. A Company was organized in San Francisco for carrying on the trade and it was known as "the Ice Company." The ice on the lake was not of sufficient thickness owing to the fact that four degrees below zero is the coldest record ever made in Sitka during a hundred years, consequently the Ice Company later transferred their chief place of operation to Wood Island, near Kodiak.

Cows were kept for milk, and the hay for their provender was cut on the Katleanski Plains on Squashanski Bay.

Sir George Simpson, Governor-in-Chief of the Honourable, the Hudson's Bay Company, visited Sitka in 1841 and in 1842. He describes the settlement, the natives, and the fur trade, and was entertained at the Castle by Chief Manager Etolin. During his stay he indulged in a Russian steam bath. His humorous description of the details ends with a promise never again to undergo such a castigation. The account of his stay at the Hot Springs is enlivened by a story of how a rosy cheeked Russian damsel, each time she passed his chair, made a profound obeisance, which he attributed to his personal attraction until he discovered her doing the same when the chair was empty, and then saw that a saintly ikon occupied a place on the wall directly over it, which dispelled the illusion. Thirteen ships were in the harbor,

---

[20] Obzor Russkikh Colonii iv Syevernoe-Amerika, Survey of the Russian Colonies in North America, by Captain-Lieutenant P. N. Golovin, pp. 72-73.

and he remarks that the bustle was sufficient to have done credit to a third rate port in the civilized world. Sir George sailed for Okhotsk on the Russian ship "Alexander," then crossed Siberia overland on his return to England from a journey round the earth.

There were eighty cannon mounted in the batteries which commanded the bay or which looked down on the Kolosh village. These cannon were of different make, some being cast in Sitka, others purchased of English or Americans, which were purchased on the ships on which they were mounted, as on the "Juno" and the "Brutus;" and other ordnance was brought from Kronstadt, Russia, as in 1804 on the "Neva," and in 1820 on the "Borodino."

Teahouses were situated on the little knoll in the center of the town where the public Gardens were located; the museum, and the library offered instruction to the workers who occupied this lonely post halfway round the world from the Russian Fatherland.

There were fourteen chief managers who directed the affairs of the Company at Sitka between the date of the founding in 1804 and the surrender to the United States in 1867.[21]

Many of the officers resided long in the colonies and their record would establish their right to be denominated as "Sourdoughs." Baranof was manager 28 years; Zarembo was rewarded in 1844 for 25 years' service; Krukof, the manager at Unalaska, was rewarded in 1821 for 40 years' service; Banner remained at Kodiak for at least ten years, and he and his wife both died there; while Kuskof came with Baranof in 1790 and returned to Russia in 1821.

---

[21] Their names and dates of holding office are as follows:
Alexander Andreevich Baranof, 1790 to January 11, 1818.
Leonti Andreanvich Hagemeister, Jan. 11, 1818, to Oct. 24, 1818.
Semen Ivanovich Yanovski, Oct. 24, 1818, to Sept. 15, 1820.
Matvei Ivanovich Muravief, Sept. 15, 1820, to Oct. 14, 1825.
Peter Egorovich Chistiakof, Oct. 14, 1825, to June 1st, 1830.
Baron Ferdinand Von Wrangell, June 1st, 1830, to Oct. 29, 1835.
Ivan Antonovich Kupreanof, Oct. 29, 1835, to May 25, 1840.
Adolf Karlovich Etolin, May 25, 1840, to July 9, 1845.
Michael Dmitrevich Tebenkof, July 9, 1845, to Oct. 14, 1850.
Nikolai Yakovlevich Rosenberg, Oct. 14, 1850, to March 31, 1853.
Alexander Ilich Rudakof, March 31, 1853, to April 22, 1854.
Stephen Vasili Voevodski, April 22, 1854, to June 22, 1859.
Ivan Vasilivich Furuhelm, June 22, 1859, to Dec. 2, 1863.
Prince Dmitri Maksoutof, Dec. 2, 1863, to Oct. 18, 1867.

Sitka in 1869–During the Time of the Military Occupation.

CHAPTER VIII
SITKA UNDER UNITED STATES RULE

Then came the day when the Russian was to withdraw from his colonies, and the United States was to occupy them as Alaska. An area as broad as an empire, equal in extent to Norway, Sweden, Finland, and Denmark combined, was to be handed over from the Imperial Ruler of all the Russias to the Republic of the United States, and Sitka, the Capital of the Colonies, was to be the scene of the actual transfer. The statesmanship of Secretary Seward, aided by the eloquence of Sumner, had secured for our country a domain one sixth as large as the whole United States.

October 18th, 1867, Alexei Pestchouroff, the Commissioner of the Tsar, appeared in front of the Baranof castle, and beside him stood Lovell H. Rousseau, the Commissioner for the United States, who was to receive the Territory.

The Russian soldiery were drawn up along the terrace which ran around the Baranof Hill, and next to them were the men of the United States Infantry.[22] The ensign of Russia was lowered, the flag of the United States raised to the accompaniment of the salutes from the

---

[22] The Russian soldiery were dressed in a dark uniform, trimmed with red, with glazed caps. The United States troops appeared in the usual full dress.

Of American ladies, six were present: the wives of General Davis, Colonel Weeks, Capt. Wood, and Rev. Mr. Rainier, of the "John L. Stevens," the wife of Mr. Dodge, Collector of the Port, and the wife of Captain MacDougall, of the "Jamestown." Six Russian ladies were also present: the Princess Maksoutoff, the wife and daughter of Vice-Governor Gardsishoff, and three whose names I do not know. H. Ex. Doc. No. 177, 40th Cong. 2nd Sess., p. 72.

batteries and of the guns of the ships in the harbor.[23] The few words of the ceremony of transfer were spoken, and Alaska became a possession of the United States.

Most of the Russian residents went back to their native land as soon as they were able to do so, but some remained to cast their lot in the land that had so long been their home.[24] Among those who remained are the Kashavaroffs, the Kostromitinoffs, the Bolshanins, the Shutzoffs, and others, whose descendants now live in Alaska.

The commanding officer of the American troops, Gen. Jefferson C. Davis, made his headquarters in the building on the hill that had been so long the residence of the Russian officers. The American soldiers were quartered in the barracks of the Siberian Battalion, and the sentries of the United States walked the beats of the Russian guards. Sitka gradually adjusted itself to the new conditions, to the crowds of adventurers who thronged its streets seeking a profit in speculations in lands and furs. They were doomed to disappointment, for the titles to lands were withheld and the fur trade was overdone, so most of the newly arrived drifted away as they came. Distinguished visitors came and were entertained in the old castle where the Commandant dispensed hospitality. Lady Franklin, the widow of the famous Arctic explorer, was once a guest at the mansion on the kekoor, and Secretary Seward was entertained there in 1869 when he visited the land he added to the possessions of the United States.

While the military garrison were content with their conditions and were not troubled with the affairs of the world at large, the civil population wished for the law and authority of other communities, and set themselves to remedy the omission of the Government in far-off

---

[23] On the lowering of the Russian ensign it caught in the halyards and a sailor was sent aloft to release it. He tore it loose and flung it down on the bayonets of the Russian soldiery.

[24] On December 14, 1807, the Russian ship "Czaritza," sailed for Russia, via London, with 168 passengers. January 1, 1868, the Russian ship "Cyane" cleared for Novgorod, Asia, with 69 soldiers of the garrison on board. November 30, 1868, the Russian ship "Winged Arrow," went to Kronstadt, but there is no record of the passengers. April 24th, 1868, the American steamer "Alexander" took special clearance for Nikolofski, Asia, to touch at all the posts along the Alaskan coasts to close up the business of the Russian American Company. Customs Records of Alaska, Record of Clearances.

The ship "Winged Arrow" sailed on December 8th, 1868, for St. Petersburg, taking over 300 persons. Seattle Intelligencer, January 11, 1869. This is the same voyage as the one above under the clearance of November 30th.

Washington so far as was possible to do, for there was no provision for an organization of civil government in the community. They organized a municipal association, drafted ordinances, elected councilmen, collected revenue for improving the Governor's Walk, changed the name to Lincoln Street, and in December opened a school. After five years the civil population declined until the revenue was insufficient to maintain the expense, the organization was abandoned, with it passed the school, and the first attempt at self-government closed.

Then followed dark days for Sitka.[25] Military rules for the garrison and no law or protection for the people. Soldiers from the fort are said to have robbed the church of its ornaments, tearing the covers from the richly bound Bible of the Cathedral. The offenders were apprehended, but there being no civil law all the punishment meted out was to be drummed out of the service and sent to the States on an army transport. The stolen property was hidden under the old hospital building and was discovered by some boys and nearly all was restored to the church.

On New Year's Day, 1869, Colcheka, a noted chief of the Chilkats who was visiting Sitka, was entertained by General Davis at the castle on the hill. The liquid refreshments served to him by the General raised his spirits and his pride of race. After it was over he descended the long flight of steps leading from the Commandant's quarters and strode across the parade ground with the dignity becoming to the hereditary chief of the Chilkats, the proudest kwan of the Thlingits. For some reason he crossed the part reserved for officers, was challenged by the sentry, and, not heeding, when he reached the stockade gate was kicked by the sentry stationed there. He was furious.

"Me, Colcheka, Chief of the Chilkats, kicked!"

He turned in a rage, seized the musket of the sentry, wrenched it from his hands, then carried it to his house in the Ranche.

The guard was turned out for his arrest and a skirmish ensued in which the guard was worsted and retreated to the barracks. The Sitkas were neutral. The Chilkats were too few in number to fight the troops, so next day Colcheka surrendered, was kept in the guardhouse for a few days and then released.

---

[25] If we may believe the current reports of the time, the military occupation of Sitka was anything but a happy time for the civil inhabitants, especially the Russians who remained. See Colyer's Report, Ex. Doc. H. R. 41st Cong. 2nd Ses., p. 1030; Seattle Intelligencer, December 14th. 1868; The Victoria Colonist, et al.

Meantime orders that no Indians be permitted to leave the Ranche were issued which were revoked upon Colcheka's surrender. Through some mistake in revoking the orders the sentries were not notified. A canoe load of Indians left the Ranche to get wood. The sentries fired on the canoe and killed two of the occupants, a Chilkat and a Kake. It was an unfortunate mistake. Those shots rang from Lynn Canal to Kuiu Island and the echoes vibrated for more than twenty years. By listening intently one might yet hear the vibrations. Two white men died and three Indian villages burned directly as a result, but it happened in places distant from Sitka, and, as they say, it is another story.

On a June day of 1877 the troops of the United States army embarked on a ship for the States and sailed away from Sitka. The buildings and property were left in charge of the Collector of Customs, who, with the Postmaster, constituted the only officials in the Territory. The presence of the military had guaranteed safety from attack by the Indians to the people of the town, and the officers had been a pleasant addition to the social life; with their departure both were lost.

The animosity of the Thlingits had been kindled by many wrongs, some real and others fancied. They saw in the new order of things an opportunity to recompense themselves for past grievances. All the old stories of the killing of their countrymen by the troops, the burning of old Kake and other villages, the loss of five Keeksitties, in the Schooner "San Diego" in Bering Sea and other tales were rehearsed and were used to stir the lust for vengeance. The Keeksittis, under the leadership of Katlean, openly advocated sacking the town, killing the men and making slaves of the women.

"The government does not care for the country. They have abandoned it. It belongs to us, anyway; why not take the town and do as we wish with it?" said Katlean.

The Kokwantons, under Annahootz, their chief, opposed the outrage. For months there was danger of an outbreak. Insult after insult was placed upon the citizens. The stockade was cut down and carried away by the Indians. Every male inhabitant was armed and expecting a call to battle at any time. A man was killed at the Hot Springs by a Keeksitty. The murderer was arrested through the assistance of the Kokwantons under Annahootz.[26] The Keeksitties assembled to rescue

---

[26] Annahootz, the friend of the whites, married his 13th wife. Afterward becoming blind and decrepit he starved himself to death. See Sitka Alaskan, February 6, 1890.

Katlean still lives at Sitka and may often be seen on the streets of the town.

the criminal, but the citizens of the town rallied for defense, the Kok-wantons joined them and the murderer was safely placed on board the Steamer "California" and taken to Portland for trial where he was afterward hanged.

On the same boat went an appeal for assistance, directed to the United States Government, but it fell on deaf ears. Another petition was sent to Victoria, B. C., and was heeded. Captain A. Holmes A'Court, of H. M. S. "Osprey," at once set out for Sitka, arrived on March 1st, 1879, anchored opposite the Ranche and trained his guns for immediate use. The danger was averted. Captain A'Court remained until the arrival of the U. S. S. "Alaska," on April 3rd, then departed for Esquimault with the blessings of the grateful people of Sitka.

On June 14th into the harbor came the U. S. S. "Jamestown." Her Commander, Captain L. A. Beardslee, assumed control of affairs in the community and administered them in a manner which brought credit on his name. He found everything at the lowest ebb; every woman and child who could leave, had gone to escape the danger of Indian massacre; witchcraft prevailed among the natives and anarchy among the whites. He took a census[27] upon his arrival, and the result was 325 people, exclusive of the Creole population. He appointed an Indian police; established more sanitary conditions in the "Ranche," numbered the houses, and compelled the attendance of the Indian children at the Mission School.

A school was opened in the old Russian barracks building on April 17, 1878, by Rev. John G. Brady and Miss Fannie E. Kellogg, of the Presbyterian Mission, which was later followed by the present Sheldon Jackson Mission School. George Kostromitinoff, afterward known as Father Sergius, was the interpreter. The opening of the

---

[27] The population of Sitka in 1818 was: Russian, 190; Creoles, 72; Aleuts, 173 of males, and female 185; of Russian and Creole, total, 620. Materialui, pt. 3, p. 20.

January 1, 1825, there were: Russians, 309; Creoles, 58; Aleuts, 33. Total, 400. Ib. p. 52.

In April, 1880, citizens by birth, 92; citizens by naturalization, 123; citizens by treaty, 229. Total, 444. Beardslee's Report, 47th Cong. Sen. Ex. Doc. No. 71, p. 34. In this census are many names well known in Alaska by the "Old Timers," as: A. T. Whitford, John G. Brady, N. A. Fuller, M. Travis, Edward DeGroff, S. Sessions, R. Willoughby, M. P. Berry, A. Cohen, Miss P. Cohen, Miss H. Cohen, Ed. Bean, D. Ackerman, A. Milletich, P. T. Corcoran, L. Caplin, Pierre Erussard, Ed. Doyle, George E. Pilz, Nicholas Haley, John McKenna, Reub Albertson, John Olds and others.

school was a great event for Sitka and nearly everyone in the town attended. Annahootz, the friendly Kokwantan war chief, made a speech. Mr. Cohen, the brewer, hunted up another interpreter to assist. Hymns were sung and the events were auspicious. The Indians stole in one at a time, some with their faces blackened, all in blankets, but they squatted by the wall and listened attentively. The school was continued until December, when it was given up, but in the spring of 1880 Miss Olinda Austin, from New York City, reopened it on April 5th, in one of the rooms of the guardhouse, with an attendance of 103 children. The school thus established was the beginning of the present Sheldon Jackson Training School. The support of the naval officers at the station was such that the missionary teacher was moved to say: "It is not often that the Government sends out a missionary, but they have sent one in this young commander and his lieutenant, Mr. F. M. Symonds," in referring to Captain Glass, who succeeded Captain Beardslee.

Some form of local government giving the residents a right to regulate their civil affairs was favored by the Commander, who had not even a code under which to act. A meeting was called, ordinances were drafted, a magistrate and councilmen elected for a town government. But all were not agreed upon these acts and opposition arose against it from the very inception of the movement. One of the traders of the town, Caplin, said: "De Captain may go to — wid his tam government; I'll bay no daxes." And from Silver Bay where he was mining, Geo. E. Pilz sent in a protest against the proceeding. The dealers who traded molasses to the Indians, from which the villainous liquor called "hoochinoo" or "Hooch," was distilled, objected to the ordinances restricting the trade. Finally an English miner named Roy was shot by his partner, "Scotty," and the inability of the self-made government to try the offender brought a crisis. The next day a notice appeared stating the organization had been dissolved, and the second attempt at self-government by the people in Alaska passed into oblivion.

Scotty was sent to Oregon for trial and was discharged because of lack of a law to punish a man for assault with a dangerous weapon in Alaska.

But the dawn of a better day was at hand, Alaska's darkest hours were past, and morning was breaking. The rule of the Navy Department continued until 1884, then, although the warships still remained in Alaskan waters, by Act of Congress of May 17th, a form of civil government was granted, and the official Capital was placed at Sitka. The terror of the Indian outbreaks was past; schools were in reach, for the same act provided for the establishment of a system of public education, and the Code of Oregon was adopted as the law of the land.[28]

Then some of the life of the former years returned to the beautiful village by the sea; there were pleasant parties among the residents, the Governor held receptions, the officers of the warships added to the social life, many a gay ball was celebrated on the top floor of the court house, and for more than twenty years it was the Capital of Alaska.[29]

With the influx of the Americans prospecting began, for in the vast wild mountains of Baranof and Chicagof Islands there is a wealth of mineral stored in the ledges.

The Russians had attempted to find the mineral of the mountains, and in 1848 a Mr. Doroshin, a mining engineer, had been sent out from St. Petersburg to search for mineral wealth in the colonies. He was not successful enough to make it of profit to them, although he found coal on Cook Inlet, gold on the Kenai Peninsula, earth promising to bear diamonds near Kootznahoo, and copper was known to be on the Myednooskie, or Copper, River.

Discharged soldiers of the garrison were the first to take to the hills with pick and shovel. Nicholas Haley, an old-time prospector of

---

[28] Governors of Alaska who made their residence at Sitka:

John H. Kinkead, of Nevada, appointed July 4, 1884.

Alfred P. Swineford, of Michigan, appointed May 8, 1885.

Lyman E. Knapp, of Vermont, appointed April 32, 1889.

James Sheakley, of Alaska, appointed June 28, 1893.

John G. Brady, of Alaska, appointed June 23, 1897.

[29] "The United States District Court, established by the Act of May 17th, 1884, was formerly organized on the 4th day of November of that year in a room set apart for the use of the court in the old barracks building at Sitka, the following officers being present: Ward McAllister, Jr., Judge; Andrew T. Lewis, Clerk of the Court; Munson C. Hillyer, U. S. Marshal; Edward W. Haskett, District Attorney.

"On the same day John F. McLean, an officer connected with the signal service, and Major M. P. Berry, a veteran of the Civil and Mexican wars, were admitted to the bar, as well as District Attorney Haskett. These three gentlemen comprised the Alaska Bar of Attorneys until June 20th, 1885, when Mr. John G. Held was added to the roll and in the month of October, 1885, Willoughby Clark, John F. Maloney, R. D. Crittenden, and John G. Brady were admitted." Alaska Bar Association and Sketch of the Judiciary, by Arthur K. Delaney.

Arizona, who came with the troops to Sitka, was one of the most energetic and daring of these. Year after year, with pick and shovel, with rifle and blankets, Nicholas attacked the rugged mountains. Rich specimens were brought in and yielded enough when brayed in a mortar to keep him in a grubstake, but it takes capital to develop a hard rock mine and capital was wary. So Nicholas toiled on year after year, keeping up his assessments and living on hopes until at last he passed over the Great Divide to a Better Diggings.

Others tried it. In 1878 a mining company was organized at Sitka, but there was not yet a law under which a claim could be legally taken. Ledges were found, small mills were placed on the ground at the Stewart Mine, the Lucky Chance and elsewhere, and later great fakes were promoted at the Pande Basin and elsewhere. But it was years after that when two Indian boys, hunting on Chicagof Island, lay down to drink at a stream, and, behold, in the shimmering water was white rock with yellow, glittering particles dancing in the clear stream. With the fear it was but fools gold they took specimens and marked the place where they were found. When they reached Sitka they submitted these samples to Judge DeGroff, and to Professor Kelly of the Sheldon Jackson School. It was pronounced to be gold, pure shining, yellow gold, and richer than the most sanguine had hoped for. After much labor and many disappointments the ledge was located from which the float came, and today that mine, the Chicagof it is called, is known as the richest and best paying mine in the United States in proportion to the money invested, and more than one fortune has been taken out of the tunnels in the mountain.

Off the shores of the continent, reaching far off to the westward almost to the shores of Asia are vast fishing grounds, perhaps the greatest in the world. A great submarine plateau stretches along shore, past the Aleutian Islands and into Bering Sea. There are estimated to be forty thousand square miles of cod and halibut banks that are known to the surveys. The fisheries of Gloucester and Cape Cod fade into insignificance and the famous Newfoundland Banks are but small in comparison.

Sitka goes back the farthest in historic memory of any city of the Northwest. When Lewis and Clarke came to the mouth of the Columbia River she was looking out over the Pacific from her stockaded walls and Resanof was sailing to search for locations for new colonies. When Astoria was founded she was placing her outpost on the Russian River in California. Before San Francisco was a city she sent her bidarkas to take the sea-otter from under the very noses of the Padres in their missions. Here the civilization of the East met the progress of the West, the Orient and the Occident met here and met without bloodshed. Sitka, with her wealth of fisheries in the waters at her doors, with her wealth of mineral in the ledges at her back, with the wealth of forest on the mountain slopes around her, is in the same latitude as Edinburgh, Scotland. The time is coming when she will have population, and wealth; beauty she already has. What more is wanted for the happiness of her people? Only energy, perseverance, and thrift, and those will be forthcoming.

CHAPTER IX
WHAT TO SEE

Approaching Sitka by the usual steamer route from the north at a distance of six miles the site of Old Sitka is passed. It lies to the left of the steamer track, in a small bay, and is marked by a native house which is visible from the ship. From near this place, looking to the westward, the first sight of Mount Edgecumbe is to be had between the islands. On approaching the town the ship goes through a narrow channel between Japonski Island at the right and the townsite at the left. Near the middle of the channel a rock is marked by a buoy and along the shore is the native village, or "Ranche," with a sloping beach upon which in former days the canoes were drawn up. The paths by which they were brought from the water may be seen, marked by the rocks being thrown to each side from the track.

Sitka–East on Lincoln Street–the Governor's Walk of the Russians.

On Japonski Island is the U. S. Naval Coaling Station and the U. S. wireless telegraph. The magnetic observatory of the Russians was situated there. The name means Japan Island and is given because Resanof designated it as the place to keep captive Japanese whom he expected to capture through his expedition against the lower Kuril Islands in 1806.

The dock at which the ship lands is in the same location as the one used by the Russians, but it has been extended to deeper water. The timbers of the old hulk once used by the Russians as a landing stage may still be seen in the water at low tide. On the dock was the landing warehouse of the Russians, a log structure with a passage through the center. It was burned in 1916. Leaving the wharf and going eastward along Lincoln Street, at the side are the booths or tents of the native merchants, kept by the women from the village, a veritable arcade of little markets, and each of the vendors is as interested as though she occupied a seat on the famous Rialto Bridge to sell the wares of ancient Venice. The picturesque, dark-skinned Thlingit women sit at the doors of their little tents hour after hour, offering the strangely carved totems, the beautiful baskets of spruce roots woven in mystic designs, the beaded moccasins, etc., products of their industry during the long winter when the tourist boats do not call at the Sitka wharves. Passing up the street to the east from the landing–at the right is the U. S. cable office, occupying the site of the old Russian fur warehouse. Next is the three-story building used for courthouse and jail, formerly the Russian Barracks where the Siberian Battalion was quartered. This is one of the most prominent of the old buildings which remain. In front of this is the stairway leading to the top of the hill on which is situated the building of the Agricultural Department, on the site of the former residence of the chief manager of the Russian American Company. Around this hill were the batteries of the Russians, commanding the Kolosh village and the harbor. The former building was often called the Governor's Mansion, or the Baranof Castle, was built about 1837 and was destroyed by fire in 1894. The hill commands a fine view of the harbor and the surrounding islands. The present structure is the headquarters of the Alaska division of the Agricultural Department. Opposite the stairway to the hill is the way leading to the "Ranche;" the open square was the former parade ground of the Army, and later of the U. S. Marines from the Man-of-War which was stationed here. East of the old barracks building is the former counting house of the Company, now occupied as the U. S. Postoffice, and during the time when Sitka was the Capital of the Territory it was used by the United States for a Customs office, and by the Governor as an office. Going east on Lincoln Street, the next large building at the right was the old bakery and shops of the Company, later commonly known as the Sitka Trading Company Building, having been occupied by that company for many years. Beyond this on the same side of the street at a short distance is a small building, standing back from the walk, surmounted by a Greek cross, which marks the site of the first church built in Sitka, in 1817. Next to this lot is the one formerly occupied by the Lutheran Church, built in the time of Etolin, and in which the first church service was held by Chaplain Rainier of the U. S. Army, after the American occupation.

Interior of Cathedral of St. Michael

Across the street is the Cathedral of St. Michael, the headquarters of the Greek Orthodox Church in Alaska. In the Territory are claimed to be ten thousand communicants of that faith and from Sitka the management of affairs is conducted. The church is in the form of a cross and is surmounted by the Greek cross. The interior is richly decorated after the usual custom of the Russian churches. Candlesticks of massive design stand at either side of the doors of the inner sanctuary. The building, with its dome, is distinctive, and is a good example of Russian church architecture.[30]

---

[30] The first church in Alaska was built at Kodiak (Paulovski) in 1795, the next at Unalaska soon after, and the third at Sitka in 1817.

Continuing east along Lincoln Street a short distance beyond the Cathedral a vacant space on the right marks the spot formerly occupied by the clubhouse, built by Etolin for a home for the clerks, navigators, and other employes of the Company–opposite it was situated the foundry and machine shops, while a little farther to the east stood the sawmills, at the mouth of the outlet to Swan Lake. Along this stream was the eastern boundary of the stockade of the Russian fort, with a blockhouse near the point of the lower end of the lake. East of this stockade were the kitchen gardens, but all traces of them have long since vanished. Continuing along the street following the shore, the Bishop's house is passed on the left, where the Russian school is taught, and a short distance beyond is the house of the Episcopal Bishop of the diocese, Rev. Bishop P. T. Rowe. Still farther to the east is the Sheldon Jackson School, the Presbyterian Mission School, consisting of a group of buildings, the first of which was completed in 1880, under the superintendence of Rev. Alonzo Austin, and others have been added from time to time until the present fine establishment has resulted. An octagonal structure shelters the Sheldon Jackson Museum, a fine collection of native work of many kinds, gathered from all parts of Alaska by the first superintendent of native schools for the Territory. A small paper is published by the mission, the *Verstovian*, and is printed by the native students of the institution.

Opposite the mission, at the edge of the curving beach, a large, flat-topped rock lies at the side of the way, called the Blarney Stone. On this it is said that Baranof often sat, during the last year of his residence here, and looked out through the vistas between the islands to the broad Pacific. What were the thoughts of the brave, strong, strange, old man as he sat here will never be known, but it is sure that there was much of sadness for him in those days.

Beyond the Mission is the famous Indian River Road, a continuation of the Governor's Walk of the Russians, and often called the Lover's Lane. It winds along the shore of the sea, through the Park, with here and there an opening in the forest where there are splendid examples of Hydah carvings in the tall totems placed in well chosen spots. These totem poles were taken to the St. Louis Fair in 1904, as a part of the Alaska Exhibit, and afterward returned to this park. One of the most interesting is the house totem of Chief Son-i-hat, of Kasaan, accompanied by the four supporting columns of the ancient tribal house.

From the rustic bridge on the Indian River there are enticing paths leading along the stream and toward Mt. Verstovia, which towers above the bay to the height of 3,216 feet. Along the river, known as the *Kolosh Ryeka*, by the Russians, the winding paths are bordered with huge Sitka spruces and giant cedars, with the space thickly filled with a dense growth of shrubbery, among which is prominent the Devil's Club (*panax horridus*), with its beautifully palmated leaves and its cruel spines concealed underneath. This shrub was formerly used by the natives as an instrument of torture in their witchcraft. In the depths of the forest the earth is covered with a carpet of ferns and mosses, and the trunks of fallen trees of former years may be seen with other trees of from two to three feet in diameter growing on their prostrate bodies.

Returning toward the town, at the Mission the Davis Road turns toward the north. It was built by the Army during their occupation, in the process of their securing wood from the forest, and named for General Jeff C. Davis, the Commander of the post. Following it the Military Cemetery is reached at the distance of about three-eighths of a mile. Here are some interesting monuments, among them being that of Gouverneur Morris, a descendent of the famous financier of the Revolution. A stone marks the resting place of a lieutenant of the U. S. Army, around whose memory lingers stories of a duel with a brother officer in a solitary spot along Indian River, over a Russian beauty of Sitka.

Turning aside from Lincoln Street at the Mission, or at the street next westward, a walk of a quarter of a mile leads to the experiment farm of the Agricultural Department of the United States. There may be seen many products, including apples and strawberries of an excellent quality. Of the latter is a variety originated by Prof. Georgeson through hybridizing the cultivated berries with the wild native berry which grows luxuriantly at many places in Alaska.

On reaching the Cathedral a street turns northward along which one finds, at the right, on the little knoll in the town, among the scattered spruce trees, the spot where formerly stood the tea houses of the Russians. They were in the center of the public gardens which covered the knoll and were approached by beautifully bordered walks. Farther along, on the left of the walk, is the remaining Russian blockhouse, the last of three which formerly stood on the line of the stockade that protected the town from the Kolosh. A little back of the blockhouse is the grave of the Princess Maksoutoff, marked with a marble slab lying on the raised mound above her resting place. At the end of the walk is the modern Russian cemetery, with its forest of Greek crosses, and in the center, at the highest point, is a platform from which is had an excellent view of the harbor, islands, Mt. Edgecumbe, and of the lake and town.

Returning as far as the site of the tea gardens, then going westward toward the water, at the right is an enclosure in which there is a small building marking the site of the Koloshian Church, or the Church of the Resurrection, as it is called in the church records. This was the building occupied by the natives in 1855 when they made an attack upon the town. It was on the line of the stockade which formerly ran from the water front at the end of the "Ranche," east to the lake, then back to the water at the sawmill. On the line of the stockade were three blockhouses, the church being between the first and second of these. Surrounding the site of the church are a number of graves, and among them are some interesting monuments dating back to the Russian days, for this is the older of the two cemeteries.

Going down to the entrance to the native town, or "Ranche," there is a choice of two streets, one in front of the houses along the water front, the other at the rear. The one at the front is preferable. The houses are built of lumber and in general are constructed by the native workmen, who have been instructed at the mission school, at which there is an excellent manual training department. The great tribal houses of former days have long since disappeared. The older houses were named by the natives much as were the inns of old England; the *Gooch-haet*, or wolf house; the *Tahn-haet*, or sea-lion house; the *Ka-hse-haet*, or cow house, and others, named for different animals. The *Kahse-haet* was named from the head of a cow being brought there from a wreck off the coast in which the animal was drowned. Formerly there were many canoes along the water front–as many as 150 at a time being often seen, but now their place is occupied by gas boats– generally built by the owners and the engines installed by them. The loss in the picturesque is partly compensated by the gain in utility, but the native canoe was a wonder of marine architecture, cut from a single log and shaped with fire and adzed into elegant lines. An occasional specimen is sometimes yet to be seen on the beach or carefully covered from the weather in some sheltered and secluded cove.

Russian Blockhouse.

There were no great house totem poles in front of the houses as there are at Wrangell, Kasaan and elsewhere. There were some mortuary columns near the grave houses which formerly stood on the ridge back of the village, but these have long been covered by the dense undergrowth which sprang up in recent years.

In this village have lived some interesting and strong characters. Annahootz and Katlean both figured boldly in the history of the town, and Sitka Jack was noted for his great potlatch held in 1877, when he gave a housewarming at which he presented to his visitors over 500 blankets, not to mention the hoochinoo and whiskey which flowed liberally for all. He beggared himself by the feast, but his reputation was established above reproach for the rest of life. Princess Tom was another celebrity, whose fame was founded on her wealth which was estimated at ten thousand dollars, and which was acquired by skill in basket making and shrewdness in dealing in native manufactures on which she was a connoisseur–going out to the villages in her long canoe to gather the stock of baskets, bracelets, carved dishes, masks, dance hats, etc., which she disposed of to advantage upon her return to

Sitka. Chief Tlan Tech was one of the prominent citizens and frequently might have been seen on the street in his frock coat, tall hat, with cane and kid gloves, cutting quite a dash. His English vocabulary was very limited and he was accustomed for many years to fly the Russian flag over his canoe when he went out to a neighboring village for a potlatch.

Some of the silversmiths were skilled workmen. Sitka Jack, and Kooska, and Hydah Jake, all fashioned bracelets, spoons, and other articles, carved with totemic designs of delicate beauty and line of proportion, made from silver coins which they melted down.

Some of the shamans of the olden time acquired great influence and made life miserable for their fellow-citizens by the practice of witchcraft. One of the most obnoxious of these, called Skondoo, was captured and his shock of matted hair, which, like that of Samson, was supposed to be the seat of his power, was shorn by the commander of the U.S.S. "Pinta," and in addition he was thoroughly scrubbed with soap and brush, perhaps for the first time in his existence.

Even to this day there are instances of the weird belief in the villages at Hootznahoo or at Klukwan. Not many years ago an Indian girl was rescued by the whites from a damp hole under a house where she had been confined to die of cold and starvation by the order of the shaman, or *Ekht*, as the Thlingit calls him.

Among the island and the inlet dented shores surrounding the town are many interesting places forming an opportunity for delightful excursions. The most desirable of these are:

Mount Edgecumbe, 3467 ft.–Taking a launch from Sitka the trip may be made to Crab Bay, or to the landing behind the island of St. Lazaria on which is a populous bird rookery, and the ascent of the mountain is possible to be made in a day. Perhaps better that two days be taken to the trip, however. The first to go to the top was Lisianski in 1804. From the summit of the mountain an unusually beautiful panorama is to be had of island-studded bay, and mountain ridges capped with glaciers on one side, while on the other spreads the expanse of the broad Pacific.

Old Sitka, and Katleanski Bay.–By launch the site of the Russian settlement of 1799-1802 may be reached and from that point a continuation of the excursion may be made to the head of Nesquashanski Bay, where the meadows are situated from which the Russians procured their provender for the cattle kept at the post. In the streams entering the bay may be seen, during the season of the salmon run, the strange spectacle of the brown bears in the role of fishermen, scooping salmon from the waters with their paws, if good fortune attend. This journey may be made in a day.

Silver Bay.—A veritable Norwegian fjord transplanted to Alaska—with picturesque waterfalls plunging into its waters, deep glacial valleys entering at right angles with Yosemite-like cliffs bordering them, the Scottish bluebells clinging to the dripping rocks which beetle overhead, Kalampy's Slide around which hangs a tale, the Stewart mine, etc.—about ten miles to the head of the bay, where a fine waterfall plunges from the mountainside.

The Redoubt and the Globokoe Lake.—Southwest from Sitka about ten miles was the location of the fishery of the Russians from which for more than sixty years they drew their stores of *krasnia ruiba* (the red salmon), which provided so important a part of their subsistence. Here in the rocky wall which divided Globokoe, or Deep Lake, from the sea, and over which the outlet flowed, channels were blasted, forming reservoirs, and in these channels were placed *zapors*, or fences, which made traps into which the salmon swam and lay in the clear cold pools until they were removed for use. Here also was one of the Russian flouring mills, where they ground the wheat brought from California, or from the farms of the Hudson's Bay Company at Nisqually or on the Columbia.

The Sitka Hot Springs.—About four miles farther to the southwest than the Redoubt, is situated the Sitka Hot Springs, possessing valuable medicinal qualities, and used for more than a century as a health resort. Here Dr. Goddard has established a sanitarium in the midst of a veritable nature lover's paradise, the forest behind, and the island-studded sea in front, with game in the deep woods and fish in the sea, all to be had for the taking.

Many other interesting and beautiful places may be visited. Lisianski Bay, Deep Bay, Herring Bay with the gorge of Sawmill Creek and the chain of lakes, Blue Lake, and others lying adjacent, are among the important ones.

Mt. Verstovia.—The ascent of this mountain comprises one of the most interesting excursions about the town. The trail leaves the shore of Jamestown Bay at the point where the trough of the watering place of the "Jamestown," came to the beach. This place may be reached by boat or on foot through the Park by the mouth of Indian River. The ascent should be under the guidance of one familiar with the route, for it is not plainly marked and none but an experienced woodsman can find the way alone. It leads through a forest, the first

800 or 1,000 feet through dense undergrowth under the trees, the mosses and ferns forming a veritable carpet; above that the woods are more open–at about 2,500 feet the forest ceases. It is called Koster's Trail. The first eminence or shoulder of the mountain is near the timber line and is often spoken of as the Mountain of the Cross, while above it towers the Arrowhead, or the summit of Verstovia, otherwise called at times Popoff Mountain, or the Ponce, to a height of 3,216 feet, nearly a Russian verst, and from this it derives its name. From the top an expanse of island-studded waters stretch toward the sea. Eastward crest after crest of glacier-capped peaks rise for a hundred miles, northward the lofty summits of Mt. Crillon and Mt. Fairweather may be seen at an elevation of over 15,000 feet, equal in height to the highest Alp of Switzerland. Around the base of the Arrowhead, in July and August, are found a myriad of wild flowers, carpeting the earth– violets, daises, cyclamen, and a multitude of others.

These are the nearer points which may be visited, but more extended journeys full of new and varied interest, to Sergius Narrows and Peril Straits or to the Place of Islands and the Chicagof Mine to the northward, and to Redfish Bay to the southward, may be made.

MAP OF SITKA–OCTOBER, 1867

Also from Benediction Books ...
Wandering Between Two Worlds: Essays on Faith and Art
Anita Mathias
Benediction Books, 2007
152 pages
ISBN: 0955373700

Available from www.amazon.com, www.amazon.co.uk

In these wide-ranging lyrical essays, Anita Mathias writes, in lush, lovely prose, of her naughty Catholic childhood in Jamshedpur, India; her large, eccentric family in Mangalore, a sea-coast town converted by the Portuguese in the sixteenth century; her rebellion and atheism as a teenager in her Himalayan boarding school, run by German missionary nuns, St. Mary's Convent, Nainital; and her abrupt religious conversion after which she entered Mother Teresa's convent in Calcutta as a novice. Later rich, elegant essays explore the dualities of her life as a writer, mother, and Christian in the United States-- Domesticity and Art, Writing and Prayer, and the experience of being "an alien and stranger" as an immigrant in America, sensing the need for roots.

About the Author

Anita Mathias is the author of *Wandering Between Two Worlds: Essays on Faith and Art.* She has a B.A. and M.A. in English from Somerville College, Oxford University, and an M.A. in Creative Writing from the Ohio State University, USA. Anita won a National Endowment of the Arts fellowship in Creative Nonfiction in 1997. She lives in Oxford, England with her husband, Roy, and her daughters, Zoe and Irene.

Visit Anita at http://www.anitamathias.com, and on
http://theoxfordchristian.blogspot.com, her Christian blog;
http://wanderingbetweentwoworlds.blogspot.com/, her personal blog, and
http://thegoodbooksblog.blogspot.com, her literary and writing blog.

The Church That Had Too Much
Anita Mathias
Benediction Books, 2010
52 pages
ISBN: 9781849026567

Available from www.amazon.com, www.amazon.co.uk

The Church That Had Too Much was very well-intentioned. She wanted to love God, she wanted to love people, but she was both hampered by her muchness and the abundance of her possessions, and beset by ambition, power struggles and snobbery. Read about the surprising way The Church That Had Too Much began to resolve her problems in this deceptively simple and enchanting fable.

About the Author

Anita Mathias is the author of *Wandering Between Two Worlds: Essays on Faith and Art.* She has a B.A. and M.A. in English from Somerville College, Oxford University, and an M.A. in Creative Writing from the Ohio State University, USA. Anita won a National Endowment of the Arts fellowship in Creative Nonfiction in 1997. She lives in Oxford, England with her husband, Roy, and her daughters, Zoe and Irene.

Visit Anita at http://www.anitamathias.com, and on
http://theoxfordchristian.blogspot.com, her Christian blog;
http://wanderingbetweentwoworlds.blogspot.com/, her personal blog, and
http://thegoodbooksblog.blogspot.com, her literary and writing blog.

www.ingramcontent.com/pod-product-compliance
Lightning Source LLC
Chambersburg PA
CBHW030518100426
42813CB00001B/84